HIPPO FOR CHRISTMAS

C.J. Carrington

Cover design by: Amos Sussigan

Illustration by: Julian Narino

Edited by: Shannon McKelden Cave

Library of Congress Control Number: 2018675309

Printed in the United States of America Copyright © 2023 C.J. Carrington

ISBN: 979-8-9894092-0-4

DEDICATION

For Connie

ACKNOWLEDGMENTS

I would like to thank Amos Sussigan, Julian Narino, and Shannon McKelden Cave for their amazing talents and generosity in helping this funky little book get made.

And, of course, Connie.

C.J. CARRINGTON

ONE

Let me begin by saying that I was a thief, and not a very good one. I was never a bad person, mind you, just unlucky. And a little misguided. I believe the difference is important. There are a lot of us unlucky, misguided people wandering the earth these days like Marley's ghost, and we can use all the help we can get.

I guess one could say getting caught was my forte, if viewed in a perverse sort of way. Poor planning matched effortlessly with poor execution and even worse follow-through—these were my talents. I believe I inherited them from my father, Howie, who was a naturally unlucky man and an even worse thief than me.

The difference between the two of us was that I stole all year round, while Howie's petty theft took place primarily during the holidays when our family's poverty was most exposed.

Not that Howie didn't have other frequent flirtations with the law, but he can write his own book. Last I heard he was in Alaska and had three Eskimo wives, which is ironic because, even as a kid, I remember his favorite joke being:

What's the penalty in this country for polygamy?

Having more than one wife!

Hah. Hah.

Why did I continue to steal when I kept getting caught?

My cellmate at the prison where I was last domiciled for over seven long years had a theory. He was a friendly fellow by the name of Carl, who fancied himself an armchair psychologist, and passed the time analyzing inmates.

Carl categorized mine as *a most intriguing case*. He suggested the key to my chronic behavior might be the diametrically opposed dispositions of my parents: Howie, whom you are already getting a sense of, and Margret, my mother, a selfless and saintly woman, who died when I was seven and my sister, Jess, was nine.

Carl says the world permanently turns ten degrees colder when one's mother dies, and Margret Spurlock was no exception. She was a wonderful woman, as well as a good provider. It's hard to imagine a more forgiving and nonjudgmental human ever walked this earth. She was the type of woman you could introduce to your lowliest of friends, knowing her heart harbored nothing but kind thoughts and warm words to all mankind. Her departure from this realm left a profound hole. Especially around the holidays.

That was when, starting in a series of consecutive Christmas Eves, Howie, a man who never met an alcoholic beverage he didn't like or a job he did, was caught and incarcerated three years in a row for Yuletide-related larceny.

Each act of criminality remains crystalline in my consciousness, and I recounted them to Carl as is clearly related below.

The first was when my father had attempted to steal us a Christmas tree. We had snuck up behind the lot and Howie had snipped the chain-link fence. I can still see him standing there with the wire cutters in one hand and a can of Pabst Blue Ribbon in the other. At five-foot five he was a short man, not tall like my mother, and with a long, peppery black and white beard. I recall a distant family member once describing him as a man who looked like he wore sunglasses to bed.

My heart beat with a rush of excitement and a blinding desire to please the old man as he handed me the small ax along with the verbal instructions, *Now, crawl on in there, Eddie boy, and get us a good one!*

Looking back on it now, I can see the plan was poor on many footings and only arrived at through the haze of Howie's constant intoxication.

Quickly, I had found a large, beautiful tree that would have barely fit through our front door and would have created a glorious sight in our barren living room. But, being small of stature, as well as thin for my age, it was difficult to bring down that behemothic evergreen in a timely manner. The police arrived before completion of my task, and they swiftly and unceremoniously took our father away.

The following year, it was a toaster oven that Howie had concluded was required to give our family a proper Christmas. But the bulky shape of the floor model under his coat made him look like a boa constrictor had just swallowed a rectangular pig. The alarming sight alerted security to what was taking place, and Jess and I watched from behind a table of men's leather wallets as our father was grabbed and wrestled to the ground. I remember the urge to run over and help him fight off the interlopers, but my sister intervened and wisely held me back.

The third and last year, we upped our game, or so we thought. Howie had devised a scheme that included a Santa suit he found at the local thrift store. I recall he and I painting a large cooking pot red in our crappy kitchen, while Jess sat in the other room with her nose in a book. She was wiser than Howie and I put together and wanted nothing to do with our criminal undertakings.

Later that evening, Howie stood on a busy downtown street corner in his Santa costume, ringing a bell, while I held out the pot to the passing crowd. It had begun to snow and there was a real feeling of Christmas in the air. I held the heavy, newly painted pot as high as I could and watched it fill nicely with small bills and change chucked in by local strangers.

All seemed to be going well, until we heard the sirens.

"Run boy!" shouted Howie as the police cruiser pulled up and slammed on its brakes.

Jess, who had been leaning against a wall reading a book twenty feet away, knocked the pot out of my hand and pulled me to safety inside a Hallmark card shop.

We both watched through the window as they stuffed our drunken Santa father into the back of the cruiser and drove off.

We woke up alone that Christmas morning to a knock on the front door. It was our Aunt Carol who had come to tell us kids that our father wasn't returning home for some time, and that we were going to live with her from now on.

That was also the day I swore off Christmas, promising never to celebrate the holiday ever again and to keep it out of my heart for all eternity.

***

I didn't see Howie much after that Christmas Eve, but apparently an impression had been made and a pattern formed, at least that's what Carl thought. His analysis went something like this: my chronic crime, coupled with the frequency of getting caught, was the result of my being stuck in a kind of self-imposed catch-22. In other words, I was simultaneously attempting to please my criminal father, while also sabotaging myself so I wouldn't disappoint my saintly mother.

Theories are great if they're working theories, but Carl's assessment wasn't much more than speculation about something beyond my limited comprehension. So, I put his diagnosis out of my mind and forgot about it.

All I knew was that I was a thief, and a bad one. And I assumed that this was my lot in life.

TWO

Eventually, when I became a grown man on my own, I continued making poor decisions that would cause no one to be proud. Such behavior had always brought a sense of distress to my sister, Jess. She had turned out more like our mother. She was the kind of woman who, if she saw a five-dollar bill on the ground, would walk away from it just to avoid any misunderstandings. Jess had married an equally honest man named Bill Strong, and together they'd purchased a failing local bar and put in the hours to get it back on its feet.

After several years of hoping I'd change my ways, I noticed Jess had transformed her concern into passive understanding and silent support. This is a state common in those who have family members whose internal compasses appear to be set anywhere but true north and are constantly getting themselves lost.

Not to say there weren't times when Jess thought I might change my ways.

One of those times was when I was nineteen and tried to rob the local bank. There was an attractive young woman working in the teller window, and she had been flirting with me from the start, up to the point that I brought out the gun, which she immediately recognized as made of chocolate. (I'd painted it black. I'm not a complete idiot.)

A rodent had gotten into the garage the night before and nibbled off the end of the barrel. I'd seriously thought no one would notice. (It's just this kind of lack of attention to detail, I have learned, that will end you.)

The teller was one of those hometown American girls, the kind with straight brown hair and fearless blue eyes. I could tell there was a strong attraction between us right off the bat. She even gave me a friendly heads up after she pressed the alarm button hidden under the counter. I thanked her for her honesty just before the two-hundred-and-fifty-pound bearded bank guard, ironically named Lil Mike, tackled me to the ground and wrapped me up in an ungainly heap.

Flora was the girl's name, and she had even attempted to help me out in court with her testimony months later, as best as she could, and without stretching any of the truth, of course. She relayed to the judge and jury how polite and non-threatening I'd been.

But neither judge nor jury seemed interested in my Midwestern manners. It was the chocolate gun they most wanted to focus on. Inquiries about the confectionery weapon were brought up repeatedly throughout the trial, and its existence may have caused many in the courtroom to question my intellectual capacity. In the end, I was given the relatively light sentence of three years.

Regardless of the outcome, I was in love and so was Flora.

After the trial, I promised her that I'd behave myself, and she promised me that she'd wait and write. We both kept our word, and when I was released one year later for good behavior, we were married immediately under her stipulation that I would give up my life of crime and get a real job.

The first several months of marriage were bliss. We got a little apartment together and lived like all typical newlyweds do in happy poverty.

But old habits die hard, and soon I found the magnetic pull to return to my old ways difficult to resist.

It started on her birthday. I was late to our little celebration at home because I was out stealing a cake for her from a local bakery. I was caught attempting to flee by way of a crawl space and fell through the ceiling tiles. (It's an occupational hazard.)

Flora was heartbroken. But she forgave me, believing that I had a good soul and that it might just take time to get it out of my system.

I was out in under a year, just in time for our anniversary. But not having a gift for the occasion and feeling embarrassed for never having had any money to buy her a proper ring, I stopped off at a jewelry store on the way home from walking her to work. Before I knew what was happening, I found myself locked in the bathroom with the merchandise on my person and the deputy pounding on the door.

After that, it was right back to prison. The real tragedy was that Flora had heard from a doctor just that afternoon that we were going to have a baby.

She was planning to tell me about the news over our anniversary dinner.

***

Luckily for us, overcrowding in the jail had me out in time for the birth. But unfortunately, when the baby was ready to arrive, Flora had to ask a neighbor to drive her to the hospital because I was doing a little late-night, after-hours shopping at The Children's Outlet Store. My heart was in the right place. I was attempting to procure all the items good parents would have in a proper nursery. I'd have gotten away with it, too, if it wasn't for a sheriff's retirement party being held in the bar next door.

Missing my daughter's birth was the last straw for Flora. Understandably, by then, her patience and mercy had worn thin, and her heart had developed a protective outer shell. She informed me that her romantic hopes and dreams had to take a back seat now. She had a child to think of, and guiding its future forward correctly meant steering it away from criminals, as well as broken hearts.

She didn't even come to my arraignment or trial in the following months. It wasn't until I was delivered by the deputy into prison, with a sentence of ten years, on account of being a repeat offender, that she appeared at the jail, alone, and informed me of her intentions.

We both cried when she said goodbye for good.

As I sat there in my orange onesie watching Flora walk away, I couldn't help but feel that I had just blown out the single candle that lit my way through a dark and lonely world.

It looked as though Howie had won.

THREE

For over seven long years of incarceration, I'd contemplated the mistakes I'd made that caused me to end up in such a desolate and lonely place. I thought about my daughter every day. Her name was Ellie, a fact I'd learned, as well as much of her yearly progress, from my sister Jess's frequent visits to the jailhouse. It was through Jess I was made aware of how the child had proved a spirited creature of great promise, learning to read at the age of three, and upon starting school, being esteemed a marvel of intelligence. *A wonder child* is how the educational system described her. The smartest student they'd ever seen, and the state tests proved it. They even skipped her two grades to keep her from becoming tainted by the pool of dummies her own age. (*Less gifted* is the term the school professionals preferred to use.)

As I continued to learn of my progeny's impressive development, I could sense a change slowly coming over me. I began to see that this small girl, who was nothing short of a miracle, had come, a least partially, from something inside me. Obviously, being the best thing I'd ever done, or ever would do, it became clear to me that I must get to know this little person and be around them, someone whom I had only heard of secondhand and had only seen in a handful of pictures.

I had already become a model member of my jailed community, biding my time until my allotted release. But now I was desperate to get out.

I campaigned to create a prisoner of the month competition and once it got approved, I campaigned again to become said prisoner of the month that month and every consecutive month after that. (An honor I proudly achieved, although I don't believe many of the other prisoners were even trying.)

My entire mental state was focused on achieving early parole.

I even got on my knees and prayed a few times, feeling it couldn't hurt, and wanting to leave no stone unturned.

But my criminal record and obvious inability to change my behavior in the past worked against me, and my requests for a probationary hearing were ignored.

The dark and lonely months continued to roll by without alteration or reason for hope.

***

A few months into my seventh year of incarceration, my prayer was finally answered, and my case came up for review.

When I went before the board, the presiding judge, an older gentleman with a shaved head and formidable mustache, asked me point blank if there was any reason they should let me out early. I rose and gave the best answer I could.

"I have a daughter, sir," I said. "A little thing, but they tell me she may be the smartest person on the planet, or close to it. I don't want to miss out on any more of her life than I already have. So, if you see fit to let me out, I promise I will never commit another crime as long as I live."

I'd been coached by my court-appointed attorney to keep my speech brief and to the point.

The other reviewers shared some words with the judge under their breath, then silently leafed through some documents in manilla folders laid before them.

It is traditional at this time in such proceedings that anyone who objects to a prisoner receiving early parole is allowed to come forward and give testimony as to why not, and this is when deputy Danny Daniels, sitting in the back of the room, raised his hand.

Now, if there is a heavy in my story, other than my own poor judgment, it's Dan. Deputy Dan and I were very well acquainted, seeing as he was the one who had arrested me more than anyone else. Deputy Dan wasn't a bad man. What makes him the heavy was only his intense dedication to his job. No man was ever more devoted to the law than Dan, and making people obey the law and bringing them to justice when they had failed was his passion.

The judge beckoned Dan forward, and he rose and walked towards the front, his large, imposing frame pushing through the little wooden gate until he stood beside me.

"Sirs and madams of the review board," he said in his usual soft voice. "I've known Eddie here a long time. We grew up together. I must have arrested him over a dozen times. And while I don't believe he's a dangerous criminal or a threat to our community, I know for a fact that he has not been forthcoming with pertinent information regarding an accomplice he had in several of his crimes. This refusal to divulge his partner's name is, I believe, a clear case of obstruction. And, as much as I like Eddie, because of this, I just don't think he's proven himself yet to be a contributing member to our community."

Dan wasn't wrong. I did have an accomplice in my last few crimes. Not that it did me any good. As unlucky as I was in getting caught, my partner was gifted in quite the opposite way and always seemed to escape.

I watched as the lead judge looked down at a sheet of paper before him. "Would this include the bank job?" he asked.

"Uh, no sir," laughed Dan. "That was clearly all Eddie. It's the crimes after that."

The judge studied the sheet again, then leaned back, took off his glasses, and rubbed his eyes. "I don't know, Deputy. This is hardly Fort Knox-level stuff," he said. "And to be perfectly honest, I kind of like the fact the man's not a snitch. I think it belies a kind of integrity and a bit of character."

I agreed with the judge on this, and although I wasn't familiar with the word "belies," I was grateful someone else felt the same way I did about the situation. But I was careful not to show it.

"Respectfully, sir," said Dan. "I don't know if I share that assessment." Dan said it with a chuckle so as not to put off the judge.

"Well, I don't care what you think, Deputy," said the judge. "The man has served over seven years and has been an exemplary inmate. I'm inclined to grant him another chance. What say the rest of you?"

In a rather surprising turn of events, it seemed as though Dan's testimony may have inadvertently swung the sentiment of the room in my favor, for the other members of the review board sitting beside the judge, either out of respect for his authority or in a desire to just avoid another late night, were inclined to agree.

"All right, so be it," said the judge. "The prisoner is granted early parole."

The judge banged his gavel, then pointed at me.

"Now don't screw this up, son," he said, "Because if you do, I can almost guarantee the next judge will throw away the key, understand me?"

Excited and thrilled by the ruling, I thanked the man and answered him in the affirmative, fully believing that my days as a criminal were well behind me, or so I thought at the time.

FOUR

It was a cold day in late November when I walked out of prison. Jess picked me up in her truck. She asked me if I was hungry and I said no, so we drove straight to the family home.

As she turned onto our street, I saw the dilapidated old structure sitting alone on the large patch of dead grass. It was really more like a large shack than a house. Peeling paint hung off the wooden sides of the front and garage. A broken window or two winked at me, as if the place was saying, *Welcome back to hell, son!*

Jess parked the truck on the street, then she glanced over at the house. "Hard to believe it's still standing," she said.

I didn't say a word as I opened the passenger side door and climbed out.
Together we walked up the porch steps. Jess took out the keys and opened the door.

As we entered, I noticed the interior hadn't changed at all. It was as barren as it had always been.

I went numb.

"Just like Dad left it," I heard her say. "TV

still gets only the one channel."

I looked around dismissively. "Yeah, well, I don't expect I'll be needing the place much," I said. "It doesn't really fit in with my plans."

Jess gave me a pitiful look. She seemed to know exactly what I was thinking.

"Yeah, about Flora," she said. "I mentioned to her you were getting out today. I'm sorry, Eddie, but she told me she wasn't interested in seeing you."

I was prepared for that bit of information and shrugged it off. "I figured," I said. "But once I talk to her, I'm hoping things might change."

A look of sadness flashed across Jess's face. She then forced a smile and for a moment she looked like our mother.

"Well, why don't we just take it one day at a time?" she said. She then looked around at the house, and her smile disappeared completely. "I really wish you had some other place to stay. Unfortunately, we just don't have any extra room above the bar."

"It's okay," I said. "It's only temporary."

Jess's smile returned, but less this time. She glanced at her watch. "Well, I better get back to work." She set the keys on the TV and gave me a hug. "I'm glad you're back."

She turned to leave. I felt like I should say something.

"Hey," I said before she could go. "I want you to know that I appreciate what you've done, keeping the house and all. I know you've been paying the property tax and all that sort of stuff."

Jess smiled. "Well, I couldn't just let the place fall down," she said. "See you tonight at six for dinner."

I thought about asking her why she couldn't let it fall down but didn't.

I watched from the doorway as she drove off. I then took a tour of the house, first the living room, then the kitchen, and finally the bedrooms. The bedroom I had shared with Jess when we were young was empty. The marks in the carpets where two beds had been on either side of the room were all that was in there.

I then entered Howie's room. I looked for the picture of Mom that had sat on the side of the bed. It was the only thing in his room I noticed missing. I assumed Jess must have taken it.

I wandered back into the living room and plopped down on the couch. I couldn't get over the fact that all the objects in the place, as few as there were, all brought up nothing but bad memories.

I had to remind myself that the past didn't matter anymore. I was focused on the future, and I was confident about what that was going to be. I reasoned that, even if Flora didn't want to see me, my daughter certainly would, and Flora wasn't the kind of woman to break a young girl's heart like that. Flora was a good person. Like Margret.

As I continued to sit there, the initial numbness from before started to wear off, and a dark cloud began to engulf my brain.

It had been such a strange feeling walking through the door with Jess after all these years. Few words had been spoken between us while she was there. Few ever were. Growing up, our father had been the talker, and mostly what he'd said was crap.

Jess had known not to listen to him from an early age, but I, unfortunately, had held out too long, hanging onto Howie's every word like a good son, hoping some wisdom might one day spill out of that fuzzy little face of his. It was, unfortunately, too late by the time I learned that nothing can pour out of something if it was never in there to begin with.

As I lay there, I could feel the yellowing walls closing in. I shut my eyes and reminded myself, once again, that this was the reason my daughter was so important. It was because of Howie that I had always assumed that I, too, had nothing good in me to pour out. But this child, a direct descendant of both me and Howie, was evidence to the contrary. She had wisdom in her. Probably truckloads of it.

And this was why I had to get to know her. I had to be there to watch, firsthand, the evidence of something good coming out of something not so good. I wanted to observe daily this miracle of advanced intelligence soaring out into the cosmos, unencumbered by the constraints of the past.

To witness this conception unconfined.

To observe this little apple falling so far from its tree.

And that was now the single goal and purpose of my life.

Of course, I knew it wouldn't be easy. I was aware that certain forces in the universe were aligned against me. Deputy Dan was a big one. I knew he had his own goal, which was to follow me day and night, watching me like a hawk, hoping to catch me in the act of committing another crime. Then he would use that against me as leverage to finally acquire the name of my old accomplice. Dan probably expected he had only to wait a few days or a week at the most before I slipped up. In his mind, criminality was in my blood, the most dominant gene in my DNA and its defining factor.

It was my life mission to prove him wrong.

FIVE

That night I had dinner with Jess and Bill in their bar. We had burgers and fries, and it was the best thing I'd tasted in a long time. I remember feeling relaxed and at ease for the first time in years.

Their place was set up like an old English pub. It had even been given a pub sounding name, "The Drowning Pig," by a previous owner years ago, although no one remembered exactly why.

While we ate, we made small talk, mostly sticking to the three distinct kinds of weather: past, present, and future. At one point, Bill told me about how the Wolverines, our local high school football team, was doing. I'd played on the team briefly in my junior year, but really had no interest in the subject, although I pretended that I did because he seemed to think it was a worthwhile topic.

We also talked about, as well as constantly commented upon, the antics of their Pug mix, Brimstone, a name acquired in jest from a chronic gastrointestinal issue. I would come to learn that, for most people, sitting around for hours observing their pets was a great source of joy and relaxation.

Howie never would let us have a pet. He said they couldn't be trusted. I imagine he was referring to the time he'd unwittingly taken in a retired police dog and the animal growled at him non-stop, presumably detecting my father's predisposition for criminal behavior.

Immediately upon my arrival at the bar, I'd noticed the talk was constantly nudged by both Jess and Bill away from the subject of my future, as well as the topic of Flora or Ellie.

I was fine with it. I understood.

But, despite their carefulness, I was still able to glean the few bits of information I needed to move forward with my plan. I may not have found out where Flora currently lived, but I was able to learn that she still worked at the bank.

All I needed to figure out was my timing and approach. I'd been working on what I would finally say to her for years. I cautioned myself to keep it simple and stick to the facts. I understood the situation did not look optimal. I'd heard many stories in prison about men stalking their ex-wives and girlfriends and how those situations all ended rather poorly. I'd convinced myself that our situation was different. I fully believed in the strength of my position and that it would be hard for Flora not to see my side of things as a rational and good person.

After dinner, I watched a little TV in the bar with the other patrons, then thanked Jess and Bill and headed home. Although I hadn't done much that day, transitioning between two very different worlds can be exhausting.

By the time I got home, I was so tired, I fell

right asleep on the couch and slept through the night.

***

The next morning, after getting ready for the day, I sat on the couch and thought about how I might approach Flora. I'd concluded that a chance meeting, an outcome of pure happenstance, should be the tone of our first encounter.

As I began attempting to conjure up a scenario that might fulfill that criterion, there was a knock on the door. When I opened it, I found a young woman standing on the porch wearing a brown pantsuit and holding a briefcase.

"Eddie Spurlock?" she asked.

"Yes?" I replied.

"I'm Lucy Alvarez," she said. "I'm your probation officer."

"Oh," I said, surprised at her young age and the fact that she was knocking on my door. At that point, I would've been surprised if anybody had knocked on my door other than Jehovah's Witnesses.

"Now, you didn't miss a meeting or anything," she volunteered. "I'm here because I like to visit my clients at their home and check out the living situation. It helps me assess things. Home environment is very important, you know."

"Sure," I said as I shrugged. "Would you like to come in?"

She smiled and entered. Once inside, she looked around. If she was horrified by what she saw, her face did a wonderful job masking it.

"Are you the only one living here?" she asked.

"Yes," I said.

She nodded then glanced around some more.

"Is that bad?" I asked.

"Not necessarily," she said. "Do you mind if we sit?" She gestured through the kitchen doorway towards the dinette table and chairs.

We entered the kitchen and sat. She pulled a file out of her briefcase.

"Now, I've looked through the stipulations of your probation, and it all seems pretty cut and dry," she said as she opened the file.

Probation was new to me. All my other crimes, before the attempt on the bank, had all been petty thefts. The bank job, because of the inclusion of the chocolate gun, was looked upon more as a sad event perpetrated by an intellectually challenged individual rather than something truly nefarious. This was the first time a probationary period had been imposed upon me.

She continued reading my file.

"It appears you weren't a part of any gang and so have no such affiliations, which is good," she said. "You have only one close family member, a sister, Jessica, who has never been in trouble with the law, so that's good. And your father, who did have quite a few run-ins with the law is 'whereabouts unknown,' is that right?"

"That is correct," I said. I didn't say anything else. I really didn't know where Howie was or if he was even still alive.

"Is your home paid for?" she asked.

"Yes," I said.

"Good," she replied.

She continued to thumb through her file. "And it appears you have a little money coming in every month from your Aunt Carol's estate," she said, without looking at me.

Sensing this might be a question, I responded in the affirmative.

"Very good, then." She looked up at me and smiled. "Well, the only other requirement that remains is for you to get a job."

Surprisingly, I was ready for this.

"My sister said I could work in her and her husband's bar," I told her.

This was the truth. Jess and Bill had offered me a job helping out at The Drowning Pig. Although I wasn't really looking forward to it, with Brimstone being a farter.

"Yes, well…" she said, "unfortunately, that's impossible. It wouldn't be compliant with the terms of your release. You're not allowed to work around alcohol."

"Oh," I said, surprised but a little relieved.

"But not to worry," she said. "I kind of pride myself on going the extra mile for my clients. I made some calls and have already lined up a prospective job for you, that is, if you want it. It's totally up to you whether you take it or not. It's available to you as an option."

I panicked. I'd never had an actual job before, where I was expected to show up and do stuff on a consistent basis. I had no idea what this mystery job might entail, how far it might be from town, or even how much time it might demand of me, time that I could be using to work on my plan. But thinking I couldn't really say no to the girl, because she had already gone to all the trouble, I just nodded and shrugged.

"Sure," I said, trying to appear as agreeable as possible. "Sounds good."

The truth is, I didn't really have a choice in the matter. There wasn't time for me to find a job on my own. Besides, I liked the way the young woman was so organized and positive. Plus, it was nice being referred to as a client rather than as a parolee. I figured I might as well trust her.

She then told me the job was at a shop on Main Street called Wayne's Pet Stop. It sold pet supplies, as well as small birds and reptiles. A man named Wayne Corbett was the proprietor. He had been a juvenile delinquent in his past but had turned his life around and now had a soft spot for people trying to get back on the straight and narrow. Lucy said he needed help for the holidays and was willing to give me a trial run if I was agreeable and could start the following Monday.

"Now, how does that sound?" she asked with an enthusiastic grin.

I told her it sounded fine. Although, to be honest, I was still a bit nervous. Not ever having a job before, I wasn't sure if I could do it. But then I realized that having gainful employment would make me look responsible to Flora. And who knows? I might surprise myself and turn out to be good at this work thing. Stranger things have happened.

Having accomplished her task, the young woman then stood and packed up her briefcase.

"I just know it's all going to work out fine,"

she said. "The trick is to always think positive and keep moving forward in service of others. That's something my father used to say. He's eighty-four and still working as a probation officer."

I smiled and thanked her, promising that I wouldn't be late for my first day of work.

After Lucy left, I wondered if she might be the kind of girl Ellie would grow up to be. Smart, helpful, and businesslike. I thought about her father and how different he must be to Howie, a man who never thought about anyone but himself.

SIX

I woke up Monday morning feeling hopeful. I put on a new shirt and pair of pants Jess had bought me for my first day of work. She was over the moon that I had a job. She even came by Sunday night and gave me a haircut on the porch. It made me feel like a little kid again.

Later, as I walked up Main Street towards The Pet Stop, I glanced across the road and was surprised to discover that the store was situated right across from the bank where Flora worked. I couldn't believe my luck. It would be virtually impossible for her not to catch sight of me at some point, either coming or going. And once she did, how could she not be impressed over how I was moving on with my life and becoming a responsible citizen?

I'd planned it so I'd arrive a few minutes early to the store, hoping I might impress my new boss.

As I stood there waiting, a large kid approached.

"You the new guy?" asked the kid.

"I guess so," I said.

"I'm Greg," he said.

I told him my name was Eddie and we shook hands.

It was hard to guess Greg's age, but he had the look of a troubled teen, with low-slung jeans and green dyed hair, which, I don't believe, I ever saw brushed. He was one of those guys who kept their Velcro wallet on a chain so no one could steal the ten bucks, at most, they kept inside it. He was an odd sort of fellow but likable. A year before, Greg had been caught with illegal exotic reptiles in the basement of his mother's house. He didn't do any jail time for it but was instead given probation and community hours. Wayne, the owner of the pet shop, hired Greg to help him get back on track, plus, he thought he'd be good at taking care of the few birds and lizards he sold in the store.

I watched Greg turn away and pull something out of his mouth. At first, I thought it might be a set of fake vampire teeth, but later learned that it was just a fancy retainer. Eventually, he'd tell me he hated the thing, but his mother made him wear it.

Five minutes later, a man with a graying ponytail and sporting a Hawaiian shirt hidden under a parka walked up.

"Well, you must be Eddie," he said. His face was expressionless, but his eyes were bright and had a kindness to them. Not a lot of people can speak with their eyes like that, but when they do you tend to notice.

"Yes, sir," I replied as friendly as I could. I immediately liked his calm but direct manner and thought I could get along with this guy.

"Good to meetcha, Eddie," he said. "I'm

Wayne."

We shook hands.

"I'll try not to let you down, sir," I said. I really don't know where that came from. I just blurted it out. I was a little embarrassed by it at first, and I glanced over at Greg to see his reaction, but he had none. He was staring at his retainer in his hand and looking like he was contemplating throwing it under a bus.

"Good enough," said Wayne. He then unlocked the door and we entered.

The interior of the shop was a little overwhelming at first, being packed wall to wall with pet supplies of all kinds. There were more objects for pets in there than I ever even imagined might exist. I would soon learn Wayne's theory on retail was to stock everything under the sun ever made for an animal or bird, in hopes that no customer would ever leave empty-handed. There must have been a million different separate items in that store, and I felt a bit claustrophobic at first, until I saw how well-organized it all really was.

Another young man came through the door. A skinny fellow with orange hair and black eyeshadow.

"Good morning, Anton," said Wayne.

Anton nodded. "I'm gonna reorganize the upper cupboards today," he said. He then proceeded to walk past us.

"I thought you did that on Friday?" Wayne asked.

"I totally bonked it," said Anton, without turning around.

I had no idea what *bonked* meant, but I

assumed it was something not good.

"All right," said Wayne as he turned back to me. "That's Anton, he mostly takes care of the stockroom. And I assume you've already met Greg."

Anton said, "Howdy," without turning around and I waved hello back.

"Well, I'll bet you're dying for the five-cent tour," said Wayne.

I shrugged and said sure, assuming that was the expected answer.

The tour lasted a good forty-five minutes. There was a lot of product, and Wayne wanted me to become familiar with all of it as quickly as possible. Since I had never used a register before, it was decided that that would be a lesson for another day. I was told my job was primarily to be always on the floor, helping customers find products or restocking the shelves when things were slow in the shop. The requirements of the job all seemed rather simple and quite easy, for which I was grateful.

At lunchtime, when I took my break, I sat on an old bench in front of the store and kept my eyes on the bank entrance across the street, hoping I might catch a glimpse of Flora.

Butterflies exploded in my stomach the moment she exited the bank. Even from across the street, I could tell she was still that same pretty girl I'd met years ago.

I watched as she turned right and headed up the sidewalk. I wanted to shout or jump up and run over to say hello. But I didn't. I just sat there quietly, eating the tuna and onion sandwich Jess had given me that morning. I knew timing would be important in our first meeting. It didn't feel right to move too fast or force anything. I decided I would wait for the right moment, one wherein having a conversation with Flora would feel natural.

It took another four days for that moment to finally arrive. Up till then I had been biding my time and focusing on the job. Patiently waiting. As I sat on the bench eating my lunch, Flora came out of the bank. But this time, instead of heading to the right as she normally did, she started walking straight across the street and right towards me.

It didn't appear that she'd seen me yet. The noonday sun, even in winter, caused a black shadow across the front of our store under the awning. It looked like she was walking in my direction for some other reason. I didn't have time to try and figure out where she might be going, because she was suddenly standing right before me. As she stepped up on the curb, I gathered my courage and stood, but not too quick, not wanting to scare her.

"Hello, Flora," I said.

She stopped to look up and see who had spoken when she recognized my face. Her immediate reaction was hard to pinpoint exactly. I like to think it was a subtle form of unbridled joy, but most likely it was just shock.

"Eddie?" she said. I could hear the surprise in her voice. She quickly smiled, recovering. "Jess told me you were…around. How are you?" She seemed taken aback, but not flustered, which was good.

Luckily, her question felt sincere and not like she was struggling to make small talk and give herself time to pick a direction to run in. I was also grateful she'd said I was *around* instead of that I had *gotten out*. It's these little details you notice in people's words that tell you who they really are.

"I'm good," I said.

"What are you up to?" she asked, her words still sounding genuinely interested and not panicked.

"I work here," I said very calmly, like it was normal for me to be working anywhere.

"Here? At The Pet Stop?" she asked.

"Yes," I said proudly.

"Well, that's great. Good for you!" she said.

There was a long silence. I needed to say something before it became even more awkward.

"How are you?" I asked.

"I'm good," she replied.

Now, I know I should have waited to ask the next question, but for the life of me, I couldn't think of anything else to say, and I was desperate to know.

"How's Ellie?" I asked.

There it was, I'd said it.

I watched as Flora's smile diminished a good twenty percent.

"Oh, she's fine," she said, as she averted her eyes by looking at the display in the window behind me. We had just started advertising a new brand of pooper scooper Wayne had recently discovered. Basically, it was nothing more than a long plastic stick with a half loop at the end to attach a bag onto. This meant you could pick up your dog's waste without having to bend over. It was called the *Poop Wand* and was already a hot-selling item. I'd spent nearly an hour that morning putting the display together. I was rather proud of how it turned out and that Flora had noticed it.

It would have been a perfect opportunity to let her off the hook by talking about the Poop Wand and forgoing a conversation about our daughter. But I couldn't do it.

"I'd love to meet her," I said.

Flora's smile now dropped away completely, possibly into negative numbers even, and she looked down, as though she really didn't want to see my face as she spoke the following words.

"Yeah, well, Eddie," she said, "unfortunately, that's a problem. You see, Ellie doesn't want to meet you."

I heard the words, but once they entered my head, they seemed to have gotten all jumbled and I couldn't make any sense of them.

"What?" I asked.

Finally, she looked up at me. "I need you to know this isn't coming from me, okay?" she said. "I told her you were around, and I asked her if she wanted to meet you…and she said no."

"What?" I asked again, feeling confused, like the conversation had just switched to German.

"Eddie, I'm sorry, really, I am," she said.

I could see it on her face. She really was in pain over this, and it made me feel bad, but I couldn't stop.

"But…why would she say that?" I asked.

"I want you to know this is not on account of anything that I have ever told her," she continued. "I haven't ever spoken a bad word about you or tried to color her view of you in any way. I knew one day you would be around, and she might want to meet you.

I've told her only the basic facts about our past, and only when she asked."

Looking back on the moment, I think I might have been having a panic attack. I remember it being hard to breathe, and my mind becoming muddled.

"But…she hasn't even met me yet," I finally got out.

"I know," said Flora with genuine pity.

I closed my eyes to calm myself. I took a deep breath. "All I've thought about for over seven years is meeting her," I said.

I opened my eyes and could see the pain on Flora's face again.

"I know, Eddie. I know. Look, I'll tell you what. I'll see what I can do, okay? But I can't make any promises. I'll ask her again."

I couldn't expect any more than that, so I thanked her.

There was another long silence.

"Well, I better get going," she said. "It was good to see you, Eddie. Really. Good luck with your new job…and everything else. Bye."

I watched as she walked up the street and my heart sank when she disappeared around the corner.

SEVEN

A week passed without word from Flora. The first three days, I spent my lunchtime on the bench. Which, at first, I thought was a good idea. I reasoned that I was making myself available for her, so all she had to do was walk across the street if she wanted to see me.

But then I realized my constant presence may have made me a little too available. Like I was making myself appear a bit like a stalker. So, I started taking my lunch in the back of the store.

Although I found it difficult not to give in to depression as I waited, I did my best to keep up my spirits. I had a lot of confidence in Flora's powers of persuasion. But even if she failed, because we lived in such a small town, it was nearly impossible not to bump into everyone at least once in a while. Eventually, Ellie and I were bound to run into each other and meet, unless she was so reluctant to see me, she went around in a giant cardboard box with two little holes cut out for eyes. But that didn't sound like anything the smartest girl in the world might do.

I even ran though several scenarios in my

head wherein I might become a local celebrity through some kind of public display of heroism and win my daughter's affection that way. Maybe a dog visiting the store with its owner might choke on one of the pig's ears we sell, and I would wrestle the foul thing out of its mouth. And maybe it would turn out to be the mayor's dog I'd rescued, and I'd be given a key to the city in a great big ceremony on the steps of town hall.

Do they still do that?

Or maybe one of the giant bags of dog food might fall off a high shelf and wing down towards one of the elderly customers, and I'd just happen to push them gently out of the way to safety. The event would obviously be documented by photograph or video by one of our other more tech-savvy customers and find its way onto the local news that evening where Flora and Ellie might see it. Ellie would say, "Dearest Mother, who is that handsome man saving the mayor's elderly mother?" And Flora would say with pride, "Why, that's your father, child." The clever girl would see what a good person I was and be overcome with pride. Then she couldn't help but want to know me personally. Of course, I would have to explain to Wayne how one of the large bags of dog food ended up on the top shelf, but I'm sure I could make something up.

I was aware that both scenarios sounded like the fevered dream of a lunatic, but I really was starting to go crazy waiting for my answer from Flora.

If anything saved me during those long days, ·it was the work. The fact is, I was actually beginning to enjoy the job. It provided me with a sense of purpose, and I liked the feeling of being relied upon. I'd gotten to know the other staff well. Greg was the wisecracker of the group, usually with a funny comment hidden under his breath, while Anton, the mysterious, creative one, was always somewhere in the back, hidden among the deep cupboards full of stock, reorganizing. I must admit, at first, I suspected Anton might be napping back there. But it seemed like every time I'd enter the stock room, I'd find hundreds of items from the cupboards had been pulled down and stacked in the middle of the floor so Anton could repack it all. Wayne, our supreme leader, as Greg called him, was always upbeat and easygoing. He was the calmest man I'd ever known.

I continued to find the particulars of the job rather easy. Even fun. Restocking was a good way to pass the time, as well as reorganizing shelves that had been left a disaster area by customers searching for that one obscure flavor of cat food. You know, the only flavor finicky Mr. Martin Van Purren might eat?

I even started to become a decent salesman, although I did sometimes find the indecisiveness of a few of our customers a bit challenging. Truth be told, there really wasn't much difference between one rubber squeaky dog toy and another, apart from shape and color, the latter of which dogs can't even see. So, when I'm asked, *Do you think my little Sabastian would prefer the green squeaky frog or the blue squeaky fish?* I'd admit I didn't have a clue. (And neither did their little Sabastian, I would suspect!)

In such situations, I usually just said whichever shape and color we had an abundance of in stock, much like a waitress in a diner might push the tuna casserole on the specials list, because it wasn't selling like hotcakes. (At least not as much like hotcakes as the actual hotcakes were selling. Which, one must assume, were always selling like hotcakes or the saying wouldn't exist.)

I do believe the job was changing me, and in a good way. Even Wayne mentioned that, by the second week, I was much more relaxed and focused.

The only real low point during those few days was when I received a surprise visit from Deputy Dan.

I was sitting on the bench on my afternoon break when Dan pulled up in his cruiser. He got out of the car and walked towards me.

Up to this point, I hadn't had much contact with Dan since the moment we'd both stood next to each other at the probation hearing. I'd spotted him around town off and on, but always from a distance. More than a few times, I'd looked up and noticed him standing across the street or on the other side of the grocery store. He would then turn and nod at me, as if to say *hello Eddie, I always know where you are.* One could not technically call it harassment, but it wasn't far off. Let's just say, as I moved around town in my normal daily routine, I felt Deputy Dan's constant presence more than the Lord's.

"Eddie," he said, as he stood there scanning the street for criminal activity.

"Dan," I replied.

"Mind if I sit?" he asked.

I nodded toward the other end of the bench, and he took a seat. His large frame made the slats dip and the buildings across the way suddenly grew two inches taller.

"Heard from Alvarez you were working here," he said, continuing to watch the street. "She informs me you not only seem to be staying out of trouble, but that you are actually doing a good job here."

I didn't know how to respond to this, or if I was even supposed to, so I didn't.

"Glad to hear it," he continued. "Transitions can be tough. Sometimes it can be hard to move on and let go of the past."

It was at this point that Dan dropped his head and stared down at the dead, squashed weeds growing up out of the cracks in the sidewalk. "Truth is, we both know this is new territory for you. Now, I'm not saying that you're like your father. Lord knows that man couldn't get straight if you ran him over with a steam roller. But I would think that, if you come clean about your past and your old partner, it might help free your conscience and help separate yourself from the man you maybe once were."

I'd known it was only a matter of time before Dan and I would be having this particular conversation. Dan was like a dog fixated on a bone that had fallen behind the couch. There was no distracting him. Not even with another bone.

I smiled at him and said, "Gee, Dan, you know the spirit of my parole requires that I leave that world behind and move forward, never looking back. I've let all that stuff in the past go. Who knows? Maybe you should leave it behind too."

Dan forced a smile. "All right," he said. He then laughed and shook his head. "I don't know how you do it, Eddie, taking the wrap like this. You're either the most loyal man on the planet, or the most gullible. I mean, what has this person ever done for you? Have you asked yourself that?"

Dan then stood. He pulled up his heavy utility belt and rested it on his hips. "Anyway, I really am pulling for you, Eddie," he said as he looked back out at the street. "I would just think that you'd want to do everything you could to move yourself forward. Not only for yourself, but, you know, for your family as well. Just remember, I'm around if you wanna talk."

I watched as Dan got back into his cruiser and drove away. I harbored no real ill feelings towards Dan. He was an honest man with a job to do. Yes, maybe he was a little too focused on some aspects of that job, but not knowing the name of my partner really was eating him alive. Part of me wanted to give him that name just to ease his suffering. Of course, another part of me wanted him to continue suffering.

It was that latter part that I chose to listen to.

EIGHT

Six days would pass before I finally heard from Flora. On a Tuesday afternoon, she'd called Jess and told her that Ellie had agreed to see me, but only under Ellie's terms. We would meet at a diner up the street and sit across from each other in a booth. The meeting was to happen in three days, on Friday night at seven p.m.

I wasn't sure why Flora hadn't called or talked to me in person. But it didn't matter. I was thrilled. Everything was falling into place.

The next two days, I had trouble focusing on work and didn't sleep much. On Wednesday, in the morning, I had another meeting with Lucy, my parole officer. She was glad to hear about my progress at the store and my getting along well with the others. I chose not to mention the meeting with Ellie. I don't know why, other than maybe I didn't want to jinx it.

Lucy informed me that I had made it into her top ten percentile of clients in the categories of adapting well, positive attitude, and overall enthusiasm. I thanked her for the high rating and gave her much of the credit.

Earlier that week, I had asked Wayne for Friday off and he agreed, so, when the day of the meeting came, I wouldn't have any other distractions. I had planned to wear the new shirt Jess had bought me, but when I woke up that morning and put it on and looked in the mirror, it didn't seem quite right. So, I headed out to the thrift stores to look for a suit.

It took me almost all day having to catch the bus to every thrift store in the tri-county area before I finally found a suit that kinda fit me and seemed appropriate. It was under ten dollars, which I thought was a fair price.

When the hour came, I left the house. It was a long, cold walk to the diner, but the brisk air helped me clear my mind and calm my nerves. As I approached the restaurant's parking lot, I spotted Flora sitting in her car and noticed she was alone. My heart stopped as I hurried up to the driver's side window, worried either she or Ellie had changed their mind.

"Hey, Flora, what's up?" I said, trying to sound calm and relaxed.

"Ellie's inside," she said. "She wanted to see you on her own."

My heart recovered. I turned and spotted a little girl through the window with long brown hair sitting alone in a booth.

As I opened the door of the diner, blown warm air and the scent of over-cooked bacon hit me, along with the sound of horrible Christmas music being ground through grease-caked speakers mounted in the ceiling.

I felt sick.

I wanted to run away.

I walked up to the booth.

"Hey there. I'm Eddie," I said. "I'm your…"

"I know who you are," she interrupted, without even looking up at me. "Sit down, please."

I stood there, frozen for a moment. I wasn't expecting such a short, succinct turn of phrase and commanding tone coming from a mere child. It was utterly freakish billowing out of her little face.

I quickly obeyed and scooted into the booth opposite her.

I must admit, it took me a moment to get up the courage to look straight at her. When I finally did, I was surprised to realize how much she not only looked like her mother, but also like her grandmother, Margret. There was that same wise and fearless expression.

We sat there in silence for what felt like a long time as she studied my face with cold, scientific disinterest.

"It's really great to finally meet you," I burbled, trying to make conversation, as well as mask my nervousness. It was shocking how unsettled she made me. She was just a child, a quarter my size, but there I sat, fearing the next word that might come out of her mouth like she was some grand universal overlord in a sci-fi movie.

"You look different from your pictures," she said sharply.

"You've seen my picture?" I asked.

"I've seen a few," she said. "My mother keeps some in a book. What's in the bag?"

I'd been so nervous I'd completely forgotten

about the brown bag I was carrying in my hand. I reached inside it and pulled out a small, stuffed puffin.

"It's just a little something I picked up for you," I said, as I handed it across the table. She calmly took it, more out of politeness, it seemed, than interest.

She held the stuffed animal in her hand at a distance and gave it a studied look.

"Is this a dog toy?" she asked.

Red shame ran across my face. I suddenly realized that I'd been so proud of the fact that I'd paid for it, rather than having stolen it, that I didn't even think about the fact that it was meant for a dog and not a child.

"Uh…" I started.

"Doesn't matter," she said setting the toy aside, placing it at the far end of the table like it was being punished for being associated with the mere mortal sitting across from her. She then glared squarely at me with a dead stare. I'm telling you there was more life left in that burnt bacon than in the look she was giving me.

"So, what is it you want?" she asked. The way she said it wasn't anything I'd expected. She sounded more like a mob boss than a little girl.

"Well, I…uh…I just wanted to meet you," I said.

"And then what?" she asked.

She was really making me nervous.

"Uh…well, I thought, you know, we could hang out. Go to the zoo or the park or, I don't know, do whatever fathers do with their kids, you know?"

I must have sounded pathetic.

"Yeah, that's not going to happen," she said.

Suddenly, I became very warm in my suit, and the shirt collar felt a size or two smaller.

"Really?" I asked, beginning to sweat. "Why not?"

"Because you can't just show up after seven years. It's not right, and it's not fair."

"But…I was in jail," I said.

"And whose fault was that?" she responded.

She had me there.

"Well, yes, that was mine…" I started. "But…"

"Do you know what that did to my mother? Do you know what she went through because you couldn't get your act together?"

I could sense real anger smoldering under her words. They said she was smart and behaved like a grown up, but I really wasn't expecting this. I suddenly felt like I was back in court before the prosecutor.

"Now, hang on a minute," I said, forcing a laugh to keep from sounding even more pathetic. "You haven't even given me a chance yet."

"Oh, my mom gave you lots of chances. She told me all about them."

"Yes, but," I said, "now, that hardly seems fair, right? I mean, she told me she didn't say anything to make me look bad."

"She didn't have to. She only had to give me the facts. I told her I wanted to hear everything. I had a right to know, and I needed to so that I could make a clear assessment of the situation and an informed decision. Don't worry, she didn't paint you in any less of a negative light than your own actions have."

I gotta admit, I was unprepared for any of this. I was floored. It really was like talking to an adult, an adult smarter than most of the adults I knew all put together. This wasn't a minor. This was Yoda in a girl's body, who could see right through me, identify all my flaws, and make a rational summation right on the spot. She was like one of those machines that diagnoses your engine while you wait.

I started to think how ironic it was to have a child you'd created that was so smart that she was too smart to be hanging out with the likes of you.

"But…look," I said. "I'm your father. Shouldn't I get a say in this?"

"No, you shouldn't. You lost that right years ago," she replied.

"But, come on…" I said, which really was the best response I could come up with at the time.

"Look, no offense," she said. "But have you ever made a good decision in your life?"

I had to think about this for a minute. Then it came to me. "I married your mother, didn't I?" I said, proud of my answer.

"Yes, but look how that turned out, how you broke her heart and left her abandoned on the very day she was having your child."

Those few words spoke volumes. Yes, I had abandoned, not only her mother, but also *her* on that fateful day.

I should have accepted defeat right there and got up and left. But I couldn't. I was not only fully committed but convinced that I had changed and was now worthy of knowing.

I felt it was time to put it on the line, to open up and appeal to her better angels. You know, look for pity. Beg. It was worth a try.

"Listen, it's…it's like this," I said. "You're all I have. That's it. I basically got nothin' else going for me in my entire life other than you. You're the thing that makes me okay, you know? I mean, I made you, right? That's gotta count for something. All I'm asking is for a chance to prove that I can be a good person."

That was it. I'd poured my heart out.

But she just stared back at me, unmoved.

It's pathetic how our children have so much power over us. It's like they're these little minions who we are supposed to be in charge of, but they are actually controlling us. What we go through to get their approval, to smile at us and deem us worthy, like members of a royal court kneeling before their sovereignty. I guess it's because we really do see them as the one chance to redeem ourselves from a lifetime of failure and obscurity.

I was now getting desperate. She had me against the ropes. I needed to throw a Hail Mary. To say something that would change the subject and get her talking. But what?

The waitress approached and asked if we were ready to order. As Ellie politely informed her that we wouldn't be ordering at this time, I glanced out the window in an attempt to reset myself. I saw a station wagon pulling into the parking lot with a freshly murdered Christmas tree bound to its roof.

It gave me an idea.

"Hey, why don't you tell me what you want for Christmas?"

She turned from the waitress and gave me a look. At first, it appeared the question had surprised her. But then she quickly recovered. "I'm all taken care of for Christmas, thank you," she said. "Besides, shouldn't you be focusing whatever resources you have on rebuilding your own life right now?"

Jeez she was tough. But I wasn't going to let it go. Most people get all weak over Christmas gifts. I was determined to get an answer.

"No, seriously, tell me," I said.

"I'm good," she answered.

I wasn't giving up. "Look, whatever it is, I can get it for you. What, you think I can't afford it? I have a job. I'm saving money. Even my house is paid for, so I can afford it." I threw that last part in about the house on account of being as smart as she was, she would obviously be aware of how home ownership is key to a successful investment portfolio.

"I'm sorry, but I think we're done here," she said.

Now I really started to panic. The smell of the bacon burning in the kitchen was beginning to make me retch. It was either that or the music, the awful Christmas music careening like a drunken sailor wandering through the establishment. It was a song I didn't immediately recognize, but it had that sappy, ear-gutting commercial Christmas sentiment so many of them do.

"Look," I said, still smiling. "I'm not leaving here until you tell me what I can get you for Christmas."

She just stared back at me. The desperation was almost too much.

"All right, I'll tell you what," I said, breaking into laughter like an idiot. "Let's make it a challenge. Tell me what you want for Christmas, and if I can't get it for you, then I'll…I'll leave you alone forever, how about that?"

I'd said it kind of as a joke, but really I had no place else to go.

"Really?" she said with some skepticism. "You promise?"

"Yes, I promise," I said.

"Okay," she said with a smile and such a tone of superiority that it sounded as though she was convinced she had already beaten me.

We sat there in silence as she continued to stare at me and think.

I started to feel uncomfortable. I asked myself what she could possibly think of that I couldn't get her? There wasn't anything, at least nothing that I could imagine.

A car? Well, she wasn't old enough to drive so that was a bit unfair, but I could do it. I'd have to buy it on credit and make payments, but I'd do it.

A house? She could have mine. I'd sign the deed over to her today.

A horse? Yes, that's got to be it! A horse! Of course! All girls love horses. I could totally buy her a horse. They don't cost that much. Unless she wanted a Kentucky Derby winner, which was unlikely. I told myself if she said the word horse, I'd just immediately say "Done!" and then we'd shake on it. The deal would be struck before she could change her mind.

I watched her little face and could see her brain working. I knew she wasn't really trying to think of what she actually wanted for Christmas, but of something that would be impossible for me to get.

Another minute went by.

I started to get nervous again. Was there some large-ticket item I'd missed? Something I hadn't thought of? Some object her near God-like consciousness could think of that mine couldn't?

I started to sweat again. Now, the smell of old coffee mixed with the bacon was starting to make me feel like I was going to pass out. And then there was that song! That horrible song! One of those dumb Christmas novelty songs that had nothing to do with the religion. I could barely hear it, but it was there, worming itself into my brain and gnawing away at my nerves like a raccoon on an open tub of Twizzlers.

I made a grimace, and she noticed, and that was it. She went in for the kill.

"Something wrong?" she asked.

I didn't know what to say. "It's that song they're playing. I...I don't like it," I said.

The answer seemed innocent enough.

We both sat silently as the song continued to play and we listened. I remembered what the song was now. It was about some horribly obnoxious little girl who was asking for a hippopotamus for Christmas. I remember somebody once telling me that, for some God-awful reason, that the song had been a huge hit in the nineteen-fifties or sixties.

Ellie listened to the lyrics as she watched me squirm.

It was then that she smiled, a real smile, for the first time since I'd sat down. It was a deep, satisfying smile, like from a cat who had just revenge-vomited in your favorite slippers. (It's a thing, I work in a pet shop.)

"I know what I want," she said.

"That's great!" I answered, trying to mask my nervousness.

"I want a hippopotamus for Christmas, just like in the song," she said.

I smiled. I could feel the tension fleeing my battered brain.

"Really?" I said, breathing a sigh of relief. "I can do that! I can get you a hippopotamus for Christmas! What size do you want?" I asked. "You want one this big, or this big?" I gestured with my hands, naively assuming she meant what any normal human would think she meant, which is obviously another stuffed animal.

She sat back in the booth and folded her arms. "No," she said. "You don't understand. Like the girl in the song, I want a *real* hippopotamus for Christmas."

I laughed, involuntarily, thinking there was no way she could be serious. I stopped and listened to the song again as the cruel and inhuman refrain played through one last time.

"Huh?" I said finally, "That's…impossible."

"You said I could ask for anything and you'd get it for me," she said.

"Yes, but…but…you're just saying a hippopotamus because you know I can't get it. You have to ask for something that I at least have a chance at getting, those are the rules."

"What rules?" she asked innocently.

I went back into panic mode.

"How about a horse?" I said. "A real horse. That's quite a challenge getting a real live horse, wouldn't you say?"

"No, I wouldn't say," she said. "Anybody can buy a horse. Getting a live hippopotamus is a real challenge. You did say you wanted to prove yourself, didn't you?"

She had me.

"Yes, but…"

"It's what I want," she said. "So, get it for me, and we'll talk. Otherwise, it was interesting meeting you and have a nice life." Then to put a fine point on it, she turned away from me, picked up her menu, and disappeared behind it.

I stared at her through the laminated images of waffles and chicken fried steaks for a long time.

"But…but…this is crazy, right?" I said.

She ignored me and kept the menu up.

"Please send my mother in. We're going to have dinner now."

I had a feeling that I could have sat there until New Years, and she still wouldn't have put that menu down.

Realizing she had officially ruled that our conversation was now over, I scooted out of the booth and exited the restaurant.

Out in the parking lot, the air was cool and clean. I approached Flora's car.

She rolled down her window and looked up at me trying to appear hopeful. "How'd it go?" she asked.

"She really doesn't want to see me. Ever," I heard myself saying.

Flora looked up at me with genuine pity. "I tried to warn you, Eddie. I'm sorry, I really am."

"Well, can't you make her see me?" I pleaded.

She shook her head. "No, I can't. I think it's important to respect her wishes, don't you?"

"But she's only a little girl," I said. "A mere child."

"Really? Did you talk to her?" she asked.

"Yeah," I said.

"Does she sound like a mere child?"

"No," I said, seeing her point.

Flora forced a smile. "Look," she said. "Maybe it's not the end of the world. Maybe when she gets a little older, she might change her mind."

"But, by then, she might be all grown up," I replied, feeling the hopelessness of the situation. "She might not need me any more at all by then."

Flora got out of the car. "I'm sorry, Eddie," she said. "I really am. It's getting cold. You better go home. I'll see you around. Okay?"

She then turned, and I watched her walk away, up to the restaurant and through the doors. I continued to watch through the window as she walked to the booth and joined our daughter. Not once did either of them look out towards the parking lot where I stood.

It began to snow.

I turned around and headed home.

NINE

I walked into my house and threw myself down on the couch, burying my face in the pillow. The blackness blocked out the light and enveloped me, and I tried to use it to numb myself from the pain.

But it didn't work because the darkness was now coming from the inside. The fire I'd built up in my soul, fueled by hope for the future and the thought of redemption, had gone out, extinguished by the honest and forthright words of an eight-year-old girl.

The odd thing was, although the encounter had been thoroughly painful, I still couldn't help but feel an enormous sense of pride over the small person that had sat across from me at the diner and mentally and emotionally pile-drove my head and heart into the floor with nothing more than her wit and power of reasoning. It was a terrible, horrible thing, I felt, that she had done to me. But she was so good at it! She was so smart, smarter than any human I'd ever known! I'd wanted to witness the miracle firsthand and, finally, I had!

As I lay there, I started to imagine what might become of such an intelligent and capable person when she grew up. Could she be a top lawyer? Definitely. She had tied me up in knots with her cross examination. What felon or white-collar corporate criminal wouldn't buckle under such intense and meticulous scrutiny?

Could she have a career as a world-famous scientist? Absolutely! Such unlimited brain power could fuel her unconditionally in any direction she chose to pursue. The world was hers.

But it was looking more and more like a world that I would have no part in.

I remembered what Flora had said, about how, one day, Ellie might be willing to let me be a part of her life, but I couldn't allow myself to go there. Who knows when that might happen? It could be years. It could also be never. Until then, I would be forced to watch Ellie progress into a superhuman from afar and read about her great achievements in newspaper clippings after the extreme light and fanfare of the moment had passed.

The darkness rushed back in like the tide.

"Oh, God!" I found myself suddenly crying out. "Why are you doing this to me? Help me!"

The outburst surprised me. I don't believe I was necessarily praying. I wasn't sure if I had the right to pray, nor the clear confirmation that anybody might actually be out there listening. All I could really do in my desperate situation was acknowledge that I would accept help from any power out there willing to lend a hand.

As I began to drift off, the thought I remember thinking most was that I wasn't sure if I wanted to reside in a world that could be so cruel and pointless.

***

I fell into a deep sleep, one from which I thought I never really wanted to wake up. I couldn't imagine anything better than to just disappear into the empty blackness of my pillow where it was safe. In that moment, it felt like light itself was the enemy, for it shone brightly on a sharp, hard-edged world that pricked the soul and left so many bleeding in the shadows of what felt like one's own nothingness.

It was Friday night, and I didn't have to go to work all weekend, so I slept. I didn't get off that couch for two days. The times when I did awake, I would clear my mind of all thought and force myself back into the safety of sleep.

***

Now, I still don't really know if there is some supreme being or super intelligence out there watching over us. But what happened next definitely would be a check in the "definitely might be" column, for I believe it was nothing short of a miracle.

It was late Sunday night when I was finally awakened by another sound in the room. At some point, I must have turned the TV on, for I heard the voice of our local newscaster, Don Packenham. Certain words had somehow broken through my protective slumber. Phrases like *shut down zoo* and *animals sold off* and finally,

… one remaining hippopotamus.

My eyes opened, and I sat up, attempting to

see the screen. I heard the newscaster hand off to a remote reporter, who then related the story of a small zoo shutting down in another county due to budget cuts. Originally, the little zoo had been funded primarily by one of the local wealthy families in town, but in recent years, the family's local factory had shut down and moved away, and so did most of the family. The city then took over the funding of the zoo. It was town pride at having the only zoo within three hundred miles that had kept the place open. But the cost of maintaining the facilities soon became unbearable, and the city council was forced to close it. They had successfully found homes at other zoos around the country for all the animals except for one: a hippo named Poppy.

As I sat in the dark and watched the local interest story unfolding on my screen, I couldn't help but feel that this hippopotamus was, obviously, meant for Ellie, and that it existed for me to prove myself to her. It was right then that I knew I would do everything in my power to get her that hippo.

Even if I had to steal it.

TEN

Of course, if there was another way to get the animal without stealing it, I would have preferred it. But after doing a little research at the library on the internet, I discovered I couldn't buy Poppy, even if I wanted to, due to local laws prohibiting the keeping and owning of animals of that size outside a zoo.

Stealing was my only option.

But how? I could tell right off this was going to be a big job, one that would probably require more than a single person.

What I needed was a crew.

***

The following morning, I was in the store stacking bags of kibble, but my heart wasn't in it. Mentally, I was miles away, plotting the delicate machinations of an elaborate heist of a large mammal.

I knew I'd need a truck or van or some kind of enclosed trailer to transport the animal. I found the little local zoo's website that listed information about

Poppy. It said that she weighed over two-thousand pounds and was just under nine feet long. She had gotten her name from the zookeeper who raised her, who had grown up in Mexico. As a baby, the hippo had a temper and her unpredictable and sometimes explosive personality swings had reminded the man of an equally unpredictable and explosive volcano near Mexico City.

Her full name was *Popocatepetl.*

I knew my challenge wasn't just in stealing Poppy, but also in keeping her, and I concluded the garage attached to the house would be perfect. Its entrance was out of sight of the street so the animal could be loaded and unloaded without being seen.

As for a crew, at least two people, possibly three, would be needed to pull the job off comfortably. This operation, and that is exactly what it was, an operation, must be planned out meticulously and executed without a hitch.

But who could I collaborate with? Who could I trust?

I'd met other fellow thieves in prison, but for one reason or another I could discount them all. I didn't even know why they would be interested in the job in first place. This was possibly the strangest heist in history. We would be stealing a large mammal with no clear value. Even the internet had no information on the going rate of hippos. Especially a hippo with a questionable attitude.

Of course, I had to automatically rule out family and friends as helpers. No one close to me could know what I was up to.

There was always my old partner in crime, but

I hadn't seen them in years. They might have moved away, or even been dead, for all I knew. I didn't think I really had the time to track them down. Plus, I didn't know if it was even safe to do so with Deputy Dan breathing down my neck.

I was stumped.

Deep down, I had this odd feeling the universe would provide. I mean, it had provided the hippo, hadn't it? All I could do was wait and see, as well as hope that the universe, if it really was now intent on helping me out, was acutely aware of the time constraints involved.

Christmas was fast approaching.

ELEVEN

Two days later, the universe supplied me with my answer.

I was on my lunch break and had been down the street at the hardware store looking at ropes and pullies that I thought might come in handy for the operation, when a man and woman walked in. I recognized the man immediately, even though I hadn't seen him in over seven years.

His hair was shorter, and his clothes were of a higher quality, as though he were now a man of means. He wore dark glasses, but I'd recognize him anywhere. It was Thomas Gaines, or "Tommy Guns," as he sometimes liked to call himself, my old partner in crime. The man old Dan was so interested in knowing about.

The sudden appearance of Tommy, the coincidence of us both being in the hardware store at the same time, seemed to fit in with how everything had been falling into place for me in my new life.

As for the woman, I didn't recognize her. She was tall and commanding, and although she had a pleasant face, there was a sternness and intensity about her that reminded me of certain German dog breeds used mostly for security. I have to admit she made me nervous.

The couple walked into the rope area of the store and stood next to me, perusing the shelves of merchandise. After a moment, the tall woman spotted my work apron from The Pet Stop, but she didn't take the time to read what it said, so she assumed I worked at the hardware store.

"You there," she commanded. "We're looking for the kind of rope a cowboy might use."

It took me a moment to realize she had mistaken me for one of the helpers. "What, you mean like a lasso?" I said with a friendly, helpful tone.

"Yes! That's it!" she cried, as though she'd been searching for the proper word all morning. "A lasso!"

It was at that point that Tommy finally glanced up for the first time and our eyes met. I could clock the panic through his sunglasses as he recognized me. He looked as though he'd spotted a ghost. Either that or his old partner, who he'd abandoned at the baby store over seven years ago.

I smiled at my long-lost friend as he continued to stare at me. He appeared transfixed, unable to move.

The woman stared at the rope, then made a face. "Yeah, I don't know," she said. "Now that I look at it, I think it's a little flimsy."

I reached down and picked out a thicker rope from the display and held it up. "Well, how about this one?" I asked. "It looks quite reliable. A rope that you can be sure would never break, no matter what." I looked back at Tommy after I'd spoken, to see his reaction.

He continued to just stare at me blankly, frozen, like he thought if he didn't move, I wouldn't be able to see him anymore.

The woman took the rope and held it, feeling its weight.

It was at this point that Tommy started to fake cough. He gestured at the latte he was holding, as if the hot liquid was choking him. He then turned and quickly ran out the door, leaving me and the woman in the aisle.

The woman turned to me and shrugged. "Yeah, I don't know if it's quite right," she said, handing it back to me. "Thank you." She then turned and walked out of the store.

I put the rope back on the shelf and quickly headed to the door. I walked outside and watched Tommy and the woman head across the street, climb into a huge, silver SUV, and pull out. I moved along the sidewalk, following their progress as they drove. I watched as they turned the corner and headed up the street into the hills. Standing on the corner, I could see the vehicle as it continued to make a left and disappear around the corner. I couldn't see the SUV anymore due to the houses, but I knew the street it was heading down.

It was a cul-de-sac.

Now all I had to do if I wanted to find Tommy was to find the house with the large silver SUV.

The rest of the day was slow at the shop, so I spent time on the computer in the back. Anton had disappeared, as he quite often did when he wasn't reorganizing. Greg was monitoring the register as usual, while reading a comic book, and Wayne was out running errands for the rest of the day.

I really should have been smarter and gone to the library to use their computer instead of using the one in the shop. Either that or learned how to erase my search history, for an hour later, while I was restocking bags of birdseed, Greg came up to me. He had a puzzled look on his face.

"Dude, can I hit you with a personal question?" he asked in his usual hip manner.

"Sure," I replied, unsure of where this was going.

"Are you, like, trying to steal a hippo?"

I nearly fell off my stepladder. I turned and looked at him. The panicked expression on my face gave me away.

His eyes suddenly went wide. "Dude, you are! You are trying to steal a hippo! Why?" he asked, sounding more intrigued than horrified.

It took me a moment to realize he'd just come from the back room and must have gone online and seen my search history.

"What? Are you crazy?" I asked, laughing and feigning ignorance.

But he wasn't buying it.

"Dude," he said, "you literally typed the words 'How can I steal a hippopotamus and get away with it?' into the search engine."

I was caught. I liked Greg, but he was a nosy kid. I think it was caused by the boredom of being stuck behind the register all day.

"What? I didn't type that," I said, pretending

to be confused.

"All right, then," he said. "So, what's this?" He held up the folder with all my notes and drawn-up plans detailing the ramps that would be required to get Poppy in and out of a van and into my garage.

I couldn't believe I'd been so careless as to leave my folder on the desk.

"Seriously, are you really plotting to steal a hippo?" he asked again. "Because if you are, I want in."

I was planning to continue denying the evidence, but his last words caught me off-guard.

"You what?" I asked.

"Dude, I'm bored off my butt in this dumb-ass town. I need some excitement. I mean, if you're planning to take out a bunch of security guards with napalm or something, then I'm definitely not your guy. But if you're really just snatching a hippo, then…yeah, I want in on that. That's like some next level business," he said.

I stared at him for the longest time, trying to figure out if he was serious. I didn't know what to say. He had all the evidence in his hands, and I could have continued the ruse and said it was just a joke or some kind of weird game I liked to play, typing wacky questions into the internet just to see the answers. But the fact was, I needed help and I'd learned over my relatively short time at The Pet Stop that Greg was basically a reliable and stand-up guy.

Not knowing what else I could do, I fessed up and shared everything right there in the back room. I told him all about Ellie and our meeting at the diner, and the zoo closing in the next county with the hippo they couldn't give away. He even agreed with me that the appearance of Poppy could be considered a miracle of sorts from God if he believed in that sort of thing.

I told him that I could only accept his help if he promised not to tell anyone, and that meant never, not even after we'd completed the heist. He'd have to be able to live with the fact that only he and I could ever know what we'd done.

It turned out he was sincere in his interest, and he agreed. We shook hands on it.

It was only then that Anton, who had fallen asleep in the storage cupboard above us, made his presence known, and insisted on joining the operation as well. Seeing as he had already heard everything, and knowing that I'd already let Greg join, I didn't think I had much of a choice in the matter.

Now I had two confirmed accomplices. The crew had tripled in size in less than twenty-four hours, but I still felt it wasn't enough for the job. Tommy owed me big. What's more, Tommy had an older brother, Ben, who owned a delivery truck for transporting huge medical equipment. It was the biggest panel truck you ever saw, and it was a dually, or double-wheeled vehicle.

I just knew that thing could carry a hippo.

My next move would be to recruit Tommy, but for that, I'd need to dip back into my criminal ways.

TWELVE

That night I had dinner with Jess and Bill at The Drowning Pig. I was in high spirits and Jess noticed and commented on it. She then told me how proud she was of me for letting go of the situation with Flora and Ellie.

I really didn't know what to say. I didn't want to lie to her, so I just shrugged and smiled. "I'm just trusting the Lord," I said, knowing the answer was kinda true and would make her happy.

It did.

It felt good having her be proud of me, even though I was knowingly deceiving her.

After dinner, and a little conversation regarding Brimstone's recently improved gastrointestinal condition, I told them I was tired from a busy day at work and said I was going home to get some sleep.

***

Once I got outside, I didn't head home. Instead, I began walking up the hill.

It was darker than usual that night, and a mist had moved in, softening the town lights. The snowmen in the square, created for our town's annual Christmas parade, looked like demented escapees from a psychiatric ward. The light from the moon twisted them into demonic shapes.

It was around ten p.m. when I made a left at the first street and headed into the same cul-de-sac I'd seen Tommy and the woman drive into two days before. The mist was even thicker up on the hill and shrouded my presence as I walked down the street like a ghost from the past.

Everything was quiet, as most people were in their homes asleep or watching TV.

I observed every vehicle parked in the various driveways. There was no sign of the large, silver SUV until I got to the very end of the cul-de-sac where the bigger houses stood.

And there it sat, in the driveway of the biggest house on the street.

I walked up to the property and looked back at the neighborhood. Seeing that no one had come out of their house and no cars had turned onto the street, I pulled a black, knit ski mask out of my back pocket and slipped it over my head. I then walked around to the side of the house near the kitchen.

I noticed some lights were on in the living room and in the kitchen area downstairs. A few more could be seen on upstairs. I peeked through the window but couldn't see anyone moving around. I grabbed a small prybar out of my coat pocket and crept up the steps to the back kitchen door. I tried the handle, just to see if it was unlocked.

It turned and the door opened.

I entered the kitchen. There was no one around, but I could hear footsteps on the second floor above me.

It was then that I had a revelation, and my revelation was this: I had no plan past getting into the house.

This was not unusual for me, as I was generally of the school of *getting inside and winging it.*

How had that worked out for me in life so far? Not well. Not well at all.

I paused to think about my next steps. I knew I needed to talk to Tommy and ask for his help. But I also knew the answer he would most likely give me, which was *no way.* The only leverage I had was his presumed shame for leaving me behind during several of our crimes, and my history of adhering to the code among thieves.

But now I felt like I needed something more to convince him. I suddenly realized that I needed to think this part of the operation through a lot more and come up with a real plan for bringing Tommy on board.

Also, I'd forgotten about the woman. It now dawned on me that I might bump into her here in the house. Right there, I decided to put off the confrontation with Tommy until another time when I had something I could really use on him.

I turned to exit, but in doing so, my prybar accidentally went through one of the windowpanes in the kitchen door. There was a loud *pop* followed by the sound of broken glass hitting the Spanish tile floor.

I froze.

I could hear footsteps rushing downstairs. I turned and opened the door to run out when Tommy came around the corner. We locked eyes, and I immediately noticed he was oddly dressed like an elf. He recognized me even with my mask on.

We stood there staring at each other for the longest time.

Finally, he spoke. "What are you doing here?!" he said in a loud whisper.

"What do you think I'm doing here?!" I whispered back. "I did over seven years in jail and never once mentioned your name! You owe me!"

We heard footsteps coming down the stairs and both panicked.

"Gretchen has guns! You gotta get outta here!" he said.

I turned to exit when Gretchen came around the corner. She, too, was dressed like an elf, or Mrs. Santa Claus, I couldn't tell. She was also holding a large, silver revolver the size of a hair dryer.

"You freeze right there!" she shouted, as she pointed the gun at me.

I froze and raised my hands. "Don't shoot!" I shouted. "I'm a friend of Tommy's!"

"Thomas, is this true?" she turned to him and asked.

Tommy stood silent for the longest time as he stared back at her with a forced grin. I could see his forehead under his elf hat begin to glisten from the sweat forming.

He shrugged. "I've never seen this man in my

life," he said.

"Tommy!" I shouted.

"All right! All right," he said waving his hands in the air. "Yes, we used to be friends. But that was a long, long time ago! I haven't seen him in years!"

Gretchen looked at the two of us. "So, if he's your friend, why is he dressed like a thief and breaking into our house?" she asked.

Tommy didn't have a good answer for that one. He just turned to me and stared.

I had to think fast.

"Well, why are the two of you dressed like elves?" I asked, thinking it might be a clever way to lighten the mood, as well as lessen the probability of gunplay.

"Because we're going to a Christmas party this weekend!" she snapped. She then started waving that hand cannon at my face. "I want to see you!" she shouted. "Take off the mask. Go on! Take it off, right now!"

I quickly pulled the ski mask off, and she immediately recognized me.

"Hang on…you work at the hardware store!" she said.

I nodded, assuming we could address the misunderstanding of my place of actual employment later, if I survived.

"Thomas, you'd better start telling me what the devil is going on!" she said.

Tommy continued to stare at her with a forced smile. He was frozen, unable to move or speak.

"Fine," she said. "I'll just call the sheriff and

have him sort this out."

Gretchen grabbed the phone off the wall and started dialing.

I watched Tommy panic. He knew I wasn't going to go down alone this time. Finally, he broke free from his catatonic state.

"Gretchen, if you call the police, there's a chance I might go to jail," he blurted out.

"And why is that?" she asked, and not in the most pleasant tone.

"Because…," said Tommy. "We…used to be…criminals together."

Gretchen took in the information with a blank stare. She then looked at me, and then back at Tommy.

She then hung up the phone.

"Well," she said, rather calmly. "One of you better start talking and fast."

***

Half an hour later, Tommy and I had explained our criminal past to his wife, how I would always grab the merchandise, while Tommy would raid the cash register, thus giving the reason Tommy always got away quicker. Having only cash in his pocket meant nothing weighed him down. Of course, he never got away with very much. At least that's what he told me. Of the three crimes we did together, I believe he got no more than a measly eighty-eight dollars and some change.

After we finished explaining our past, Gretchen paused for a moment, then gave me a stern look. "All right, then," she said. "You still haven't explained why you're here, breaking into our house. Are you after money, is that it? Cause I guarantee they'll throw the book at you if it's blackmail you're after."

"What? No!" I said, horrified at the thought. "I'm not here for blackmail!"

"They why did you break into my house?" she asked.

"Because I need help," I said.

"Help with what?"

"With a job," I said.

"What kind of job?" she asked, suspiciously.

There really wasn't any reason to beat around the bush.

"I'm going to steal a hippo," I said.

Ten minutes later, I had relayed the entire story. I told them everything, including the part about the hippo most likely being a miracle. I didn't mention that I'd already acquired two other accomplices. But not knowing if Gretchen and Tommy were going to join the operation, I reasoned the less they knew about the crew the better. Plus, my accomplices, with their lack of experience, weren't really going to help sell the idea to them anyway.

When I was done telling them everything, I waited for their response.

"So, what do you think?" I asked nervously, hoping they would both say yes.

Tommy started shaking his head.

But Gretchen just stared off into space. She had this look in her eyes, like her mind was suddenly far away.

Now, I should probably give you a little backstory on Gretchen Bluth, Tommy's wife. This is all information that I was to discover many years later, but I believe it helps to explain what happened next.

Gretchen grew up a banker's daughter in a small town, which is kind of like being the preacher's daughter or the sheriff's daughter in a small town. It's not really a coveted position, because everyone around thinks you're purer than a dozen Sundays and can't be very interesting, let alone much fun. Because of the pressure Gretchen felt growing up to always be above suspicion, quite early on, she began fantasizing about becoming a thief, and her greatest fantasy was to hit her father's bank.

At first, Mr. Bluth, Gretchen's father, thought it was kind of cute hearing a little girl dressed in pink ribbons and bows talking about robbing banks. But as Gretchen got older, he grew concerned, especially when she started drawing up elaborate plans explaining how she would pull off such a job and get away with it.

Desperate, the man began plying his daughter with everything she'd ever wanted to coerce her to stop. Eventually, Gretchen learned to use this leverage to her advantage and blackmail her father for anything her little heart desired.

But the dream of being a criminal never really dies, it just goes on the lam for a time. There was rarely a store Gretchen ever entered that she didn't think about how she might take out the cash register, locate and crack open the safe, or extract the most valuable piece of jewelry from the case undetected.

One could say it wasn't really in her nature to be a thief, but it was definitely on her mind.

A suspicious person might even surmise that she had possibly detected Tommy's criminal background and that that is what drew her to him. I mean, I guess he may have had what they call a rakish charm, although I'd say it bordered more on weasel than anything else.

In any case, Gretchen was not only on board with stealing a hippo, but she was also ready and willing to fund the entire operation, despite Tommy's pleas against it.

I had my crew.

THIRTEEN

The next day was December eighteenth. Which meant the team only had a week to plan and pull off the operation.

I was aware that for this to be a proper Christmas gift, we would need to have Poppy in our possession no later than Christmas Eve. Any time after that and we were risking the possibility of Ellie crying foul, claiming I'd failed to get the present to her within the accepted time frame.

So, it was crucial to get this thing up and running ASAP.

Two days later, we had our first crew meeting. Feeling that I had already worked out most of the plan in my head, I was excited to share it with the crew. But knowing that Deputy Dan was probably still watching my every move, I realized the meeting couldn't take place at my house. What made the most sense was to hold it in the rear of The Pet Stop after hours. Greg, Anton, and I would already be there, and Gretchen and Tommy could slip in through the back door off the alley.

At six in the evening, after the last customer

had left the shop, Greg locked the front door. We kept the lights on to make it look like we were staying late to do inventory. At five after six, Gretchen and Tommy gave the secret knock on the alley door, and Anton let them into the back room. Greg and I joined them.

Wayne was out of town at a pet supply convention, so we knew he wouldn't interrupt us with a surprise visit.

I cleared everything off the desk in the middle of the room, then pulled several small items from the shelves to represent our persons, as well as elements of the heist. These I would use to illustrate my plan in miniature. I used several boxes of bird-beak sharpeners to create the fence around the zoo, as well as the back gate, where Poppy had been relocated from the original hippo area.

Since the rest of the zoo was now closed, they'd altered one of the monkey cages near the main offices close to the rear of the zoo to hold her. This kept Poppy near the remaining skeleton staff, so they could keep an eye on her and easily feed and clean her grounds. A small basket was used to represent the van, and various chew toys placed inside it would stand in for the team. The reverse end of a Poop Wand made a perfect pointer.

"This is the fence and the pen where they keep Poppy," I said, as I moved my pointer around. "I've checked the area out, and it's all pretty straightforward." I moved my pointer along the side of the desk. "We'll drive up here towards the back around ten p.m. and park under this embankment of trees. The gate we'll break into is here."

As I pointed to the box of bird-beak sharpeners, Gretchen raised her hand.

"Yes?" I said.

"What kind of lock is on that gate?" she asked.

"What?" I asked. "Uh, I don't know. Just a lock."

"Well, is it a lock in the door?" she asked. "Or is there a padlock or chain on it?"

"What?" I said as I shrugged. "I dunno, I couldn't get that close."

She was starting to get on my nerves.

"How about security?" she asked.

"There's a guard," I said. "But he always takes a thirty-minute break at 10:15 and goes home for a late dinner, so we'll—"

"No," she said. "I mean cameras. Are there any security cameras?"

I gotta admit I was getting a little frustrated with the twenty questions.

"Well, maybe," I said. "I dunno. It doesn't really matter because we'll all be wearing masks."

"Yeah, that's a bad idea," she said. "Masks are no good."

"What?!" I said, with a little attitude. "Why not?"

"Uh, because the latest security software can recognize a person's posture as well as guess their exact height and weight," she said, a little too snooty for my liking. "It can also identify idiosyncrasies in the way you walk or move your body."

Okay, now this woman was really starting to annoy me. I looked over at Tommy, hoping he might pull her aside and ask her to let the professionals work. But he just averted his eyes from me.

"Look," I said to her. "I appreciate you wanting to help out and all, but whose heist is this?" I said it thinking it would put her in her place and end the pesky questions.

"Well, it's your heist," she said. "But that doesn't mean the rest of us all want to end up in jail."

The nerve of this woman!

"Well, maybe you'd like to plan it yourself?" I said, again thinking I might get a totally different response than the one I got.

Immediately, the rest of the team raised their hands and chimed in with agreement. Apparently, they not only thought I was making a recommendation, but that I was also putting it to a vote!

I must admit I was a little taken aback.

"No offense, Eddie," said Greg. "But I'm pretty sure she could do this a lot better. She did go to college, and her dad does run a bank."

I looked back at my team as they stared at me. I could see in their eyes they were all in agreement.

"She is actually really good at planning stuff, Eddie," said her husband, the weasel, without even looking up at me. "Maybe you should just let her do it."

Now, I may not be the sharpest brush in the drawer, but I immediately detected a problem here. A military general sending his troops into battle needs to have those troops one hundred percent behind him, or else the battle is already lost.

I knew I had to make a quick decision here.

Any delay would jeopardize our time frame. And where would I find another crew as quickly as I found these guys? So, I gave in. I shrugged and said, "Sure, I get it." Then, graciously as I could, relinquished the Poop Wand over to our new leader.

Gretchen took the pointer and began. It turns out she already knew there were cameras on the gates, because she and Tommy had scoped the place out on their own the night before. They had driven to the zoo and taken photos of the gate, and the guardhouse, and the trees and everything in the surrounding area down to the last acorn.

Gretchen then pulled out her laptop and proceeded to play a twenty-minute-long PowerPoint with photos and videos going over every detail of the plan.

There might have even been a pie chart or two in there.

After the presentation, everyone sat speechless for a moment. Then they broke into a loud round of applause.

Gretchen looked up at me for approval. The look on her face wasn't so much smugness as it was pride.

She had the crowd on her side. What else could I do but join in with the applause?

***

Later, after we'd let Gretchen, Tommy, and Anton out the back door, Greg and I went back into the main store to finish closing. As he added up the register and I swept the floor, I realized that I was still feeling a little uneasy about no longer being in charge of my own heist.

I turned to Greg. "Hey, be honest," I said. "What do you *really* think of Gretchen's plan?"

Greg stared at me in silence, choosing his words wisely before he spoke.

"Well," he said. "I think it's concise, well thought-through, and easily executable with minimal exposure or risk. In short, I think it's brilliant."

Deep down I knew he was right. It was definitely way more thought-through than my plan. The added touch of throwing pillowcases over the security cameras was utter genius.

"Yeah," I said. "I guess it is brilliant."

I must have sounded a little down because Greg came over and patted me on the back.

"But do you know the best thing about the plan?" he said.

"No, what?" I asked.

"No one would ever suspect that you came up with it," he said. "You know, in case things go south."

I had to think about this for a minute before I got his point.

"Yeah, that is a good thing, isn't it?" I then said, smiling.

Suddenly, I felt not only okay about the plan, but actually quite good about it. Greg was right, if we got caught, no one would ever suspect I was the guy behind it. Plus, having Gretchen in charge also meant I could focus on other things, like how I was ultimately going to present the hippo to Ellie, a part of the operation I hadn't yet spent much time on.

There was a knock on the door causing us both to jump. We looked out the window and saw Deputy Dan's round face looking in at us through the glass.

I panicked. "What do you think *he* wants?" I asked.

"Heck if I know," answered Greg.

"Well, do you think we have to open the door for him?" I asked.

"It might be a little suspicious if we don't, seeing as how he's looking at us," he said.

"Good point," I replied.

I walked to the door, unlocked, and opened it. I could feel my palms suddenly become sweaty against the metal door handle.

"Hey, Dan," I said, smiling and trying to keep my voice steady and sounding like I hadn't just been plotting a major crime.

Dan entered.

"Noticed your closed sign wasn't showing like it usually is," he said. "Then I saw the light was on. You guys open late tonight?"

"My bad," said Greg. "I must have forgotten to turn the sign over."

Dan started looking around. "A little late for you guys to be working, ain't it?" he asked.

I could hear the suspicion in his voice. I hoped he hadn't walked by the alley earlier and seen the others slipping out the back. I never was very good thinking on my feet. I didn't know how to respond. Thank goodness for Greg.

"Just doing some extra inventory," he said. "We got a big shipment of dog and cat Christmas costumes coming in tomorrow, so we thought we'd better move some merchandise around to make room."

"Oh, yeah?" said Dan, sounding like he may have half bought it.

"Yes, that's true," I said, feeling like I should say something.

Dan glanced around the store. I imagined he was looking for an overturned cash register or possibly a blown safe.

"Where's Wayne?" he asked.

"At the pet supply convention in Dawson," said Greg. "He went to get more merch for last-minute holiday shoppers."

"Hmm," said Dan as he continued to look around. "He does like to pack this place, doesn't he?"

Dan then turned and stared at the open back-room door. It was then that I remembered we hadn't put the props for the operation away, not to mention all my drawings and plans. I knew that if Dan walked back there and saw that stuff, he would be full of questions.

My heart jumped and I presume Greg's did too. But he didn't show it.

"Hey, Dan," he said. "We just got some of those chewy pig's ears in. You know, the one's your dog likes?"

It worked. Dan stopped looking towards the back and turned around.

"Oh, yeah?" he said, as a grin appeared on his face for the first time. "Yeah, ol' Timber loves those things. He can go through one an hour like a buzz saw."

Dan started walking towards the front. I breathed a sigh of relief.

Greg pulled a box of ears out from the shelf behind him and set it on the counter.

"Unfortunately, the register is closed," said Greg. "But if you want you can just take a couple for the ol' boy and just pay later. We know you're good for it."

Dan looked at the ears in the box. He then looked up at the both of us and smiled. "Well, I appreciate that," he said. "But I don't mind coming back when you're open officially."

He then took one last glance around the store.

"Well, better be on my way," he said. "Got rounds to do. You fellas have a safe night and stay warm," were his last words as he turned and disappeared out the door.

Greg locked the bolt behind him, and we both breathed freely again.

FOURTEEN

Over the next three days, the store was busier than ever. Flora stopped by a few times, mostly just to pick up little gifts for her parents' dogs. It may have been wishful thinking on my part, but I started to wonder if she might have been coming in just to see me. We'd bumped into each other a lot around town in the past week and always stopped to have a quick chat. In those brief moments it kind of felt like old times. I could imagine she might have been impressed with my ability to move on with my life and accept Ellie's decision, like it appeared that I had. She must have thought it showed a great deal of maturity on my part.

I don't know if any of that was true, and there was no time to really contemplate it due to the frenzy of the holiday chaos happening all around us, but we seemed to have a moment or two of general affection in those few chance encounters. I couldn't help but start to believe that there might have been a change going on in Flora's heart regarding her feelings about me.

As the holiday approached, the town started

moving into full swing, getting ready for the annual Christmas parade.

This was the other reason I hated Christmas, other than my father.

Our town was famous throughout the tri-county area for doing Christmas big. I mean, really big. Like on-steroids big. Bottom line, if you loved Christmas, this was the town you'd want to be in come December 24th. But the reverse was also true. If you hated Christmas, then the 24th in our town, as well as the month leading up to it, were nothing but pure hell.

Every day, more and more Christmas-themed paraphernalia would appear up and down Main Street. From elaborate snowflakes hung from every lamppost to giant elves made of wire and holly standing on all the street corners. Cranes, blocking traffic, constantly moved up and down the street, hanging lights, and bunting, and great big silvery Christmas balls.

The old fire engine, no longer in use, had been brought out of mothballs, and one of the local farmers had hooked up his horses to pull the old thing down the street. They did a couple of test runs midday, and people on their lunch breaks stopped to wave at the ancient, withered fighters of the flame, who came out of retirement to balance on the historic vehicle's back end. They played second fiddle to the red menace himself, Santa Claus, who sat in the catbird seat on the front, hogging all the accolades from the crowd. Mind you, I'm talking about a man who never put out a fire in his life, but, on the contrary, encouraged people to put dying trees in their houses and wrap them with shoddy electrical wiring.

Or worse, cover them with candles.

For someone who disliked the holiday as much as I did, these preparations were not unlike some ancient, trickle-based water torture. It was all I could do to force myself not to think about what was going on around me and, instead, focus on my work and the operation at hand.

***

In the final days before we closed the shop for Christmas Eve, the place was total bedlam. Products flew off the shelves as quickly as we could restock them. It was Wayne's aggressive purchasing, as well as Anton's hours spent packing, unpacking, and repacking the back cupboards, that saved us and kept our customers from revolting. Every time they panicked, thinking we were out of some item, Anton would find another unopened box stashed away somewhere in the back, whether it was in the rafters or in the walls or even in the under-sink cabinet in the employee bathroom.

We never ran out of a single item or turned away an unsatisfied customer.

***

Thursday finally arrived, the day before Christmas Eve, and the night of our operation. The shop had been especially busy that day with what felt like more traffic than we'd ever had.

At the end of the very long day, after the last

customer had finally exited and Greg had locked the front door, we all breathed a sigh of relief. In a real Fezziwig moment, the shop then had our own Christmas party.

It was a small affair. There were punch and cookies, and Wayne handed each of us an envelope. Inside it was a bonus check and a letter thanking us for our hard work, as well as informing us that we were all getting a raise in the New Year.

We all thanked him and toasted each other for surviving the holiday. It was a nice moment.

After our short celebration, I had some last-minute straightening to do, and as I finished up, Wayne came up to me. By then, Greg and Anton had already left. They would be getting ready to head over to the operations rendezvous, while Gretchen and Tommy would be on their way to borrowing the van from Tommy's brother.

Wayne grabbed my hand and shook it. "I'm proud of you, son," he said. "I know it's only been a month, but I can already see a change in you. I know what we do here isn't rocket science, but I can tell you take the work seriously and genuinely care about the customers. That's really the key, isn't it? Thinking of others."

I nodded and agreed with him as I checked the clock on the wall above his head. It was ten minutes after eight. I still had plenty of time to get to the rendezvous.

"Spending the holiday with your sister?" he asked.

"Yes, sir," I said.

"Good, good," he said.

I didn't know how long this was going to last or if I should say something.

"How about you?" I asked.

"Oh, I usually spend the holiday helping at the food kitchen. It's always an interesting time," he said. "Sometimes they even let me play Santa Claus."

I nodded politely. I didn't know what else to say. I kept having to fight the urge to look up at the clock again.

He then handed me the keys. "I want you to close up shop tonight," he said. "Be here early Monday morning, and we'll get you up and running on the register, give poor Greg a break."

Wayne wasn't a big talker, and that was a lot of words for him to say at one time. But the word that stuck out and made the biggest impression on me was *register*. He was going to allow *me* to run the register, to sit high on the stool at the front of the store and oversee the money. It was an overwhelming feeling to suddenly realize how much a near stranger trusted me and that I'd earned that trust. It was a warm feeling. I have to say I liked it.

Wayne then said goodbye and exited out the front door. I watched him through the window walking up the street. All bundled up in his coat and hat, I couldn't help but think he made a pretty good Santa Claus.

I was about to lock the door when it suddenly flew open, and someone walked in.

It was Flora.

She smiled at me. "I was hoping I might catch you before you left," she said. "Are you all done for the night?"

"Just closing up," I said.

"You have any plans for dinner?" she asked.

It wasn't just the words that blew me away but the way she said them so casually. Like it wasn't any big deal she had just asked me to have a meal with her.

"Tonight?" I said, trying to sound not in shock. "Uh…no."

"Ellie is shopping with her grandma, and I have at least an hour if you want to grab something quick. Unless you have other plans…"

I stared at her blankly. I couldn't believe this was happening. It was my dream. I almost forgot about my hectic schedule that evening.

"What me? Other plans? Of course not," I said. "Just give me a second to make sure the back door is closed."

I ran to the storeroom and checked the door, then, quicker than the dickens, finished the lock-up routine.

It wasn't like I'd forgotten about the operation, but, in that moment, I really thought I could have a quick dinner with Flora and still make it to the rendezvous in time. I mean, it wasn't like I was going to turn down Flora's invitation. I had no way of knowing if she'd had a real change of heart about me as I'd hoped, or if it was just that weird, temporary state people get into around the holidays. You know the one, where they forget about stuff like who they hate or don't trust or who failed them and decide to welcome everyone indiscriminately back into their hearts and homes again?

I joined Flora outside and suggested we go

somewhere close. We decided on the little burger joint around the corner. It was a place we used to frequent when we were first married.

The place was packed, but we found seats at the outside counter. The owner had put up a thick, clear plastic sheet over the patio and had mounted heaters in the ceiling, making it warm and cozy inside.

After we ordered, we sat quietly watching the last-minute shoppers walking up and down the street. It felt like old times, and I was enjoying myself so much that I stopped checking the clock on the wall behind me every five minutes.

A little later, after we'd finished our burgers and ordered a slice of cheesecake to split, Flora looked over at me and smiled.

"I've been wanting to tell you something," she said. "I've been thinking about our situation."

The word *situation* surprised me. I didn't know we had a situation, but I was glad to hear we did.

"Eddie," she said, "I don't think Ellie has really given you much of a chance."

"Oh?" I said, not sure where she was going with this but liking the way it had started.

"I know you'll be spending a lot of time with Jess and Bill in the next few days, but I wanted to invite you to come by my parents' place on Christmas Day. Even if it's only for five minutes. I think it would be nice."

You can imagine how stunned I was. I stared at her face and thought she could not have looked more like an angel.

"But what about Ellie?" I asked.

At this, she shrugged. "It's my parents' house," she said. "They can invite whoever they want. And they agree with me that Ellie should give her father more of a chance."

My face remained calm, but there were fireworks going off in my head so big and loud that I couldn't see or hear for a moment. I couldn't even think. That was all I'd ever wanted, a chance to spend a little time with Ellie to prove that I could be a good father, and now everyone was supporting me and thinking it was a good idea. Even Flora's parents.

I tried to speak, but nothing came out. A tear formed in my eye. Flora saw it, but I didn't care. She smiled and looked down, not wanting to embarrass me.

I had to turn away to collect myself.

It was at this moment that I saw the clock on the wall and noticed it was 9:32. We'd been sitting there well over an hour, and I was now forty-seven minutes late to the rendezvous.

FIFTEEN

How could this have happened? I thought. Panic set in.

I hopped off the stool. "I…I just remembered I forgot to check the water bottles in the animal cages back at the shop," I said. "I'm so sorry."

"It's all right," said Flora, smiling. "Will I see you tomorrow night at the parade?" she asked. "I know it's not really your thing, but it might be fun hanging out drinking hot chocolate and stuff. Ellie and my parents will be there."

I took out my wallet and put down enough cash to cover the bill. "It sounds nice," I said.

She then leaned over and kissed me on the cheek before I could leave.

"See?" she said. "Christmas miracles do happen."

In an evening of many wonderful surprises, the kiss was the biggest. It was warm and kind and the best thing I'd felt in a long time.

***

Quickly I walked up the street and around the corner. I pulled the burner phone that Gretchen had given me out of my pocket and tried to dial.

But the phone wouldn't turn on.

It was then that I remembered I'd failed to plug it in the night before to charge it.

I now went into full panic mode. I needed to stop my team from going through with the operation. There was no need for Poppy now that Flora had invited me back into her life. Having a stolen hippo around would only complicate things.

I pulled out my regular phone and turned it on. I knew Gretchen had said not to use it to contact the other members of the team, but I didn't have a choice. It was an emergency. I tried to find Gretchen's number, then realized I didn't have it. The only number I had for any of them was in the burner phone. My only option was to run home, plug the burner phone in, and get it working.

At this point, the parade preparations had gone into full swing, and now I couldn't go up Main Street, because it was blocked off. I had to go the long way round the high school, which would add twenty minutes to my journey.

I started running.

By the time I'd made it to my street, thirty-five minutes had passed, and I was out of breath. If the plan had gone forward successfully, they would be starting back from the zoo with Poppy about now. I had to stop them.

But then I thought, *what if the plan had fallen through?* Maybe because I'd failed to show up at the rendezvous, and they couldn't reach me by phone, they'd abandoned the whole thing and instead went out for ice cream? Ice cream was the most innocent thing I could think of. Everybody liked ice cream.

I made it to my front porch and unlocked the door. I ran inside the house and furiously searched for the charger. I found it in the cushions of the couch and plugged it into the wall. I jammed the cable into the phone and waited for it to turn on. It felt like forever before the lights on the screen popped up. I pressed on Gretchen's number and waited as it dialed. There was a long moment of silence, like the phone was still trying to wake up.

Finally, a sound came through the line.

But it wasn't a ring tone, it was a dead sound.

I dialed the numbers of the other members' burner phones. But I only got the same result. This led me to two separate conclusions: either all the members of the team had failed to charge their burner phones, or they had already turned them off, pulled out the batteries like Gretchen had taught us, and dumped them.

I fell back onto the couch to think, as well as catch my breath. As I laid there, I reasoned that it wasn't plausible that they all could have forgotten to charge their phones. So, they must have dumped them, which I tried to reassure myself was a good thing. What made the most sense to me, or what I wanted most to believe, was this: that once I had failed to show up at the rendezvous or contact them, they presumed something had gone wrong and wisely abandoned the operation. This was clearly the most rational thing to do and would explain the dead ring tones.

I decided to accept this scenario because it's the one that would result in the least number of life complications moving forward.

Finally, I started to relax. I thought back on what an amazing day I'd had. First with Wayne giving me a raise and a bonus. Then, with his making me feel like an official member of the team who could be trusted to handle the money. Greg had already been showing me how to use the register out of boredom, and it really wasn't that difficult.

It was truly incredible how my life had changed so much in a matter of weeks. I never thought I'd have a real job, let alone be good at it and have fellow workers who I liked and who liked me. I was part of a real team. And although I know some people might think selling pet supplies wasn't such an impressive thing to do with one's time, I would disagree. Pets are an important part of people's lives. A lot of our customers are alone, and their dog or cat, or ten dogs or cats, or hamster or parakeet or goldfish or whatever, were the only constant companions they had. Just think of how much lonelier the world would be without pets?

I was proud of what we did.

I then thought about the dinner with Flora and the kiss. How she seemed to be like her old self again, sweet and bubbly and kind. Being back in that warm light sure was wonderful.

I was on top of the world at that moment, feeling better about myself and my future than I ever had. The universe really seemed to be smiling down on me. And to think it was all happening at

Christmas. Maybe I could learn to like the holiday a little. Or at least learn to tolerate it.

Suddenly, I realized how tired I was as my eyes became heavy and began to close.

It was then, as I peacefully drifted off to sleep, that I heard the loud thump coming from my garage.

SIXTEEN

It was later that I would learn from Greg the details of the following series of events.

At eight in the evening that night, Gretchen and Tommy had left their home and driven to Tommy's brother Ben's house. His van sat out back with the keys in it, just as Ben said it would. As had always been the case between them in the past, Tommy didn't tell Ben why he wanted the van and Ben never asked.

They'd driven the van to the rendezvous point in the field just outside of town behind Randall's Lumber and arrived on time. Greg and Anton showed up to join them seconds later.

The four of them then waited for me ten minutes past the official meeting time. When I still hadn't shown up, they tried to call me on my burner phone. When there was no response, they were unsure of what to make of it.

They then waited another ten minutes, and when I still hadn't shown up or answered my phone, they took a vote on whether they should scrub the whole operation.

It's hard to describe the condition of a human's brain in the moments leading up to a big heist, but it's accurate to say one finds oneself in a heightened mental, physical, and emotional state that is hard to come down from. The adrenaline, pumping like hot lava through one's veins, is so strong that it takes an incredibly disciplined person to turn away from it.

Knowing this, and knowing, too, that stealing a hippo for a little girl for Christmas, an unhappy hippo, mind you, that nobody wanted around anyway, had to be one of the best things anyone could ever steal, which made it an even harder opportunity to walk away from.

I mean, it was practically a victimless crime. Right? Anyone could see that.

It was this fact, along with the four of them not wanting to miss out on being involved in what might have been the most monumentally exciting thing they would be a part of in their entire lives, that caused the vote to go quick and be unanimous.

The four of them had decided that, with or without me, they were going to steal a hippo.

***

From that moment on, the plan had gone off like clockwork.

It took them exactly thirty-eight minutes to get to the zoo as per Gretchen's schedule. They didn't even have to wait for the guard to take his break. As they drove up to the trees they'd planned to park under for cover, the guard mysteriously came out of his little shack half an hour early, got into his car, and drove off.

Realizing this might be their only chance, the team sprang into action.

Anton snuck down the side of the fence and threw pillowcases over the security cameras. Greg approached the gate and cut through the lock with a battery-powered grinder. The two of them then pushed the doors open wide enough for Tommy to back the van in. It took Tommy a couple of tries to roll over some thick tree roots that stuck up out of the ground, but once he did, the back of the van buffeted up nicely against the gate to Poppy's pen.

Tommy opened the back of the van, and he, Greg, and Anton pulled out and set up the reinforced ramps used, normally, for rolling up heavy medical equipment. Tommy then removed the hook from the gate and slowly opened it. He and Gretchen peeked in and saw Poppy standing about twenty feet away in the middle of the compound.

Greg and Anton brought out the bags of mini melons, which, with a close eye on Poppy for any sudden movement, they carefully placed on the ground leading to the ramp. They then scattered the rest of the melons around the back of the van.

Gretchen stood by silently with a stopwatch, dressed in all black and orchestrating every step with hand signals from her long, praying mantis-like arms.

The team all stood by and watched as Poppy got the scent of the melons and started moving towards them. Once she found the first one, it took her only a few minutes to eat her way to the ramps, where she spotted the remaining melons sitting inside the van. As she started moving up the ramp towards the other melons, everyone's eyes were on the steel bracing. They knew that if it didn't hold, Poppy would fall, and the operation would be over, ending in failure.

There would be no other way to get her into the van.

Luckily, the ramps' integrity maintained, and, slowly, she made her way up into the middle of the vehicle. The chassis creaked a bit as she moved around inside, but the overall superstructure held.

Slowly, they closed the van doors and locked her in. Tommy and Gretchen then jumped into the cab, and Tommy started it up and gently drove forward. He was able to maneuver around the roots this time by driving closer to the guard house so as not to cause the van to rock and rattle the contents.

Once the van had driven out, Greg and Anton closed the gate to the pen and to the back entrance. Gretchen hopped out of the cab and pulled a padlock out of her backpack, one that matched the one Greg had cut through. She had purchased it through the dark web so it couldn't be traced. She then placed it on the gate and locked it. The guard would never know it was a different lock from the original until someone tried to open the gate the next day.

When they were out of sight of the cameras, Anton snuck back down the wall and removed the pillowcases. He and Greg then climbed in the cab, and the van drove off.

It was the smoothest theft of an unwanted hippo that had ever taken place in the history of the world.

***

Driving back to town, the team hit almost no traffic, causing them to make even better time. Once they'd reached my neighborhood, the delivery went just as smooth as the pickup. Tommy drove the van around the back of the property and backed down the hill towards the garage. Greg and Anton got out of the cab and opened the garage door. They pulled the plywood barriers around from the side of the house and set them up. These I had built earlier that week to Gretchen's specifications.

Once they got the barriers up, Tommy opened the back panel doors. Poppy stood inside looking out at them with remnants of crushed melon dripping from her mouth. The floor of the van was covered in squashed rinds and the cause of their destruction was now looking for more. Quickly, yet carefully, Tommy and Greg slid the ramps out and set them up.

Once they were in place and supported, Gretchen and Tommy dumped a large burlap sack full of fruit in the center of the garage and quickly got out of there. Poppy immediately spotted the fruit and moved down the ramp. In no time, she was standing in my garage. The barriers were pulled away, and the ramp was taken up. Greg and Anton began dumping more fruit from burlap sacks into the garage near the door. A rather large stack of fruit built up before they were done. They then closed the garage door and slid the clasp into place, locking Poppy inside.

They all climbed back into the van and took off. The phones were burned, the van was returned, and everyone was back in their homes safe and sound by ten thirty.

SEVENTEEN

At first, I assumed the sound coming from the garage must have been nothing more than a raccoon that had somehow gotten in. But upon hearing it again, I realized it was far too loud to be a small animal.

Whatever it was, its rustling was causing the whole house to shake.

I jumped up and ran to the kitchen. I unlatched the top of the Dutch door to the garage, opened it, looked inside, and there I saw Poppy, standing in the middle of the cement floor where Howie used to park his Rambler.

It was the first time I'd seen her in the flesh. From her stats on the zoo website, she may have been listed as smaller than your average hippo, but she had the appearance of the full-size model. She was enormous. I stared down at her in awe as I watched her popping melons in her teeth like they were balloons. When she'd back up to shovel a new melon into her mouth, her rear end would bump against the garage wall. This was where the loud sound was coming from, as well as the shaking of the timbers.

I couldn't believe it. Not only had the crew pulled off the operation, but they'd accomplished it in less time than the schedule had called for. And as surreal as it was to have a hippo in my garage, I couldn't help but feel Poppy looked quite at home, having a snack, nestled alongside Howie's workbench and the old water heater strapped to the wall.

It was then that I was struck with a strange emotion. The only way to describe it would be as an overwhelming sense of accomplishment, accompanied by an odd feeling of elitism. I could safely say that no one else in town, let alone in the entire tri-county area, had one of these babies in their garage. It filled me with a weird sort of home pride.

It dawned on me that I now had a major decision to make. Ellie had given me an impossible task to fulfill, and, surprisingly, I had accomplished it. The problem was, I didn't need the hippo anymore. Flora was now on my side. All I had to do was not screw things up moving forward and everything would go my way.

Of course, it was hard not to want to tell Ellie about Poppy and let her know that her father had successfully accomplished the herculean task she'd assigned him.

The question then arose, could I guarantee what Ellie's response would be? Would she be impressed and honor her promise, allowing me back into her and her mother's lives forever? Or might she see this as the perfect opportunity to get rid of me for good?

I suddenly realized that, if Ellie knew about Poppy, I would be totally at her mercy. All she had to do was tell Flora I'd stolen a hippo, or even make an anonymous call to the sheriff's department, and I'd be toast.

Would she really do that? My own flesh and blood?

She might. She was a very determined young lady. I had won her mom back, it seemed, but I hadn't yet won my daughter over. She might think she needed to protect Flora from me.

I could imagine the scenario: standing in their living room, Ellie would pick up the phone and dial the sheriff and then turn to Flora and say, *"It's for the best, Mother. Trust me, one day you'll understand."*

I gazed down at Poppy making short work of a melon. I wondered what she must be thinking about all this. Was she happy to be on a little adventure? To be doing new and exciting things? Maybe she hadn't even noticed her change of environment. Maybe she didn't even care. All she cared about were the snacks.

I remembered Gretchen had said that I must always have plenty of fruit around for Poppy to eat, or else she'd get restless and go looking for it elsewhere. I glanced over at the two large, colorful piles near the garage door. For now, it seemed she was well stocked and probably had enough to last her through early Christmas morning and her scheduled release.

At that time, around four a.m., I was to quietly open the garage door and let her wander out. She would then, hopefully, make her way through the neighborhoods while everyone slept until somebody finally noticed her and called the zoo to come pick her up.

It would ultimately have been only a short time she was away from her home. Less than forty-eight hours.

Of course, this would mean that, if I wanted to share the existence of Poppy with Ellie, I would have only Christmas Eve to do so.

As I continued to watch Poppy eat, a sadness suddenly came over me. Looking into the eyes of that two-thousand-pound animal, I believe I recognized a kindred spirit. I knew what it was like to feel alone and excluded in a world that appeared to move in harmony without you. Like a beetle born inside a clock, clueless as to where it fit in.

I leaned down and picked up a melon that had rolled over to me and sent it back to her. She lowered her face and scooped it up, crunching it and sending parts of broken melon everywhere. Her eyes continued to watch me as I rolled two more stray melons in her direction.

In that moment, it felt like we'd established a bond. Like we were one. I even thought, what if I hadn't really freed Poppy just to get back into my daughter's life? What if the moment I saw her on the news I'd recognized her pain, and that's really why I broke her out?

It's no fun going through this world alone.

The altruistic angle was a nice thought, but ultimately a sad one, knowing that, regardless of why I broke her out of her prison, I was eventually going to be the one to send her back there.

Life isn't always fair. All we can do is make the best of it.

It was then that I decided not to tell Ellie.

Having the issue resolved, all I really wanted to do at that moment was sleep, but I was still enjoying being in Poppy's presence. Something about her large shape made me feel at peace, like standing next to a mountain or a large body of water. Sometimes things bigger than us can make us very calm.

I sat down on the floor and rested my head on the doorjamb as I continued to watch her, and she watched me.

I drifted off.

***

Later, I awoke on the couch. I must have moved there at some point and turned on the TV, because I could hear the voice of Don Packenham of channel 4 news. I opened my eyes and was surprised to see a picture of Poppy on screen. Don threw to his remote reporter, who then told the story of how the guard at the zoo had returned after his break to discover Poppy was missing.

The sheriff, having played back the zoo's security video, noticed a ten-minute blackout in the recording.

They concluded that Poppy must have been abducted.

The unusual nature of the crime led the authorities to assume that this was nothing more than a prank, possibly pulled off by a college fraternity or some other sort of group for a laugh. Having no current leads, the zookeeper, along with the sheriff's department, put out a joint public statement demanding Poppy's quick and safe return.

I wondered if other members of the operation had seen the news.

I wondered if Ellie had seen it.

Part of me secretly hoped she had.

I didn't know if I should be concerned by the fact that the authorities were now aware of our crime. I concluded that panicking would only make things worse, I was still going to release Poppy at four in the morning on the 25th regardless. Then, by the time someone spotted her, I would have removed all evidence of Poppy's short stay in my garage.

It was a perfect crime. I doubt the sheriff's department would even continue the investigation. They might haul a bunch of fraternity boys in from the local colleges and give them a good talking to, but when was that ever a bad thing? Those kids probably did something they should get raked over the coals for.

The incident would then, most likely, be forgotten. People might even start making jokes about it, saying that Poppy had let herself out just to go on a brisk holiday walk through the tri-county area.

Everyone would have a nice laugh.

Seriously, who in their right mind would steal a hippo?

As I'd said before, it was a perfect crime.

EIGHTEEN

I woke up late the following morning, showered, and checked on my hippo. She was standing exactly where I'd left her the night before, still voraciously munching away on her food. I'd heard that sharks never slept and had to keep constantly moving to survive. I wondered if it might be the same with hippos. Only, instead of moving, they stood still, eating fruit. Either way, she seemed happily preoccupied with her melons, so I let her be.

Now that I look back on it, I can see that I probably should have checked the piles of fruit to see how much she'd devoured in the night. But I guess my mind was preoccupied, most likely on the evening ahead when I would be hanging out with Flora and Ellie and Flora's parents at the Christmas parade.

***

Not having to work at the shop that day, I casually headed down to The Drowning Pig around noon to help Jess and Bill get ready for the evening's events. The Christmas parade was a big deal for the bars and restaurants along Main Street. Huge crowds from all over the tri-county area and beyond would cram onto our downtown sidewalks and overflow our establishments. It was a huge year-end boost for the local economy and all the proprietors strove to put on the best show of hospitality and blatant in-your-face Christmas spirit in hopes of getting a little free publicity from the news crews covering the annual event.

I spent the afternoon filling the large urns of hot mulling spices and ciders set on the bar and helped Bill make sure the dozens of kegs were lined up in the basement ready to go for the revelers.

At around five p.m., we had a quick dinner. It was an hour until the parade started officially, and Jess was already nervous about the number of customers expected to pass through the bar that night. She kept asking Bill questions to make sure that they were ready for anything. Underneath her stress, I could tell she was actually quite happy. The bar had had a great year, it was Christmas, which, unlike me, she loved, and the latest turn of events with Flora had made her cry tears of joy. The fact that there might be a slight chance of us getting back together thrilled her.

I couldn't remember a time I'd felt more positive about my future, even though I had a ton of hippo contraband in my garage.

It really seemed like everything was going my way.

***

At 5:45, I finished my dinner and headed out to meet Flora in front of The Pet Stop. As I made my way up the street through the packed crowd of parade watchers getting ready for the festivities, I noticed that, for the very first time in my life, I felt like I belonged, like I wasn't a stranger in my own town. I knew I was making a lot of assumptions, mainly that Ellie would see the way Flora and her grandparents were treating me that night, and it would force her to change her mind about me. I even imagined the evening might end like one of those TV Christmas movies, where everyone wraps up the night arm in arm with cheers of *Merry Christmas and God bless us, everyone*!

Even the poor, unlucky saps like me.

As I approached the shop, I saw Flora and her parents standing on the curb. Flora was wearing a red dress with a red bow in her hair. She looked so very pretty. Ellie was there, too, standing off to the side, getting ready to watch the parade.

I walked up and said hello to everyone. They all greeted me cordially.

Except for Ellie, who never even turned around to acknowledge me.

I was unfazed by this. In fact, I totally understood where she was coming from. Her mother was breaking the promise she'd made and was forcing her to spend time with her father.

At that moment, I really wanted to tell her about Poppy and that I had accomplished a miracle. But then I remembered that I'd promised myself I wouldn't.

We heard some bells ringing, announcing the

parade was getting underway, and we all turned to look up the street.

A marching band started things off. As they passed by, I glanced over and observed the joy on Ellie's face as she reacted to the band and everything else coming up the street. As advanced for her age as she was, she was still a little girl, thrilled with the pageantry and spectacle of this strange thing called Christmas. I looked around at the crowd and saw the exact same joyful expression on all their faces. There was such wonder in their eyes over the town's transformation into a whole Christmas-themed world of bright colors and familiar carols.

I gotta admit, I still didn't get it.

Another band and then some clowns and acrobats came up the street and marched by us. As many in the crowd struggled to get a better position to see the antics of individual performers, I was slowly being pushed to the side until I found myself standing next to Ellie.

The crowd applauded as a group of young people dressed as snowflakes appeared, prancing down the street, spinning and twirling with their arms spread as wide as they could, acting as though they were being tossed about on the wind as they fell to earth.

It was at this point that I thought I might say something to Ellie. I couldn't see the harm in it. She seemed to be having such a good time, and she was standing right next to me.

I leaned down and said, "I'll bet you'll make a great snowflake one day."

I thought it was a rather nice thing to say, but

apparently not. Because it was then that she looked up at me for the first time with her little face that was intelligent beyond its years and said, with a calmness that bordered on serial killer, "I want you to listen to me very carefully. I don't care that you've somehow wormed your way back into my mother's heart. I will never accept you as my father, and I will never want to have anything to do with you. Do you understand?"

It took my brain a moment to register the words she'd said because of the noise all around. But it was primarily the expression on her face that had made her point quite clear. It was an expression of pure hatred coupled with cold, undeniable resolve.

Suddenly, I realized that she had actually been nice to me when we first met at the diner. There, she'd treated me like a professional, like anyone you might meet for the first time, even if you were only meeting them to tell them that you didn't want to work with them. But the kid gloves were off now, and this was her telling me how things really were.

I stood there, frozen. It felt like a knife had been plunged deep into my chest, cutting me open. I didn't know what to do or what to say. I wanted to disappear, to get out of there, to shrink down into the pavement and escape that intense and grown-up stare of hers.

"I got your hippo," I heard myself blurting out.

I couldn't believe I'd said it. I promised myself I wouldn't, but there it was.

She looked up at me with an annoyed expression. Because of the loud crowd, it was obvious she hadn't quite heard what I'd said.

So, I said it again. Loud and clear.

"Your hippo," I repeated. "I have it back in my garage. I didn't bring it with me because I didn't know if you opened your gifts on Christmas Eve or Christmas Day."

I thought my little joke would make her laugh, but I watched as her expression turned from cool disdain to outright contempt.

"Now you're just being pathetic," she said.

I gathered she hadn't seen Don Packenham and the late-night news.

I watched as she then slipped between her grandparents and disappeared behind them, using them like her own, personal fortress of solitude.

I tried to shrug off the incident. I turned and looked over at Flora. Luckily, she hadn't witnessed the exchange. She caught my eye and smiled at me. I was able to force a smile back at her.

But I was wounded.

I turned back towards the street and tried to pretend the short conversation between Ellie and me hadn't happened. I tried to get interested in whatever was now moving past us on the parade route. But I couldn't, because there was a nagging feeling deep inside me. It was a feeling telling me that something was wrong. Very wrong. And it wasn't with Ellie or the situation.

It was with me.

It's hard to explain what happened next or why. It was as if someone had switched a lightbulb on in my head. Images started flooding in of a future where every day was made more painful and awkward simply by my very existence; a world wherein my presence undermined the delicate and special balance Flora had built with our daughter. I saw Ellie growing rebellious and angry like I had been as a teen. I saw Flora becoming frustrated over her daughter's unwillingness to accept me. And all of this because I insisted on sharing in their wonderful little world, a world I had no part in creating, but was now forcing myself into.

It felt as though a heavy curtain had parted, exposing some ugly scene in an old play, wherein I was a mustache-twirling villain wearing a top hat. As I watched it play out in my head, the image of Howie danced naked across the stage like a little medieval jester. As he moved around in my mind, I realized the dark spiral I'd allowed myself to get caught in, caused by my thinking that I needed to make the weird old man proud of me.

How much better, I suddenly wondered, would my life have been if he just hadn't been there? Or if I had just ignored him like my sister Jess had?

In that moment, it became clear to me how I had been using Howie as an excuse for my own bad and selfish behavior, as well as my loneliness.

I didn't want to live in that world anymore, and I didn't want Ellie to be forced into a world that was in any way like that.

Tears fell from my eyes, and I used my hand to quickly remove them so no one would notice.

I believe this is what they call an epiphany or self-revelation. Both terms I'd learned from my cellmate, Carl.

Ellie had tried to tell me that she wasn't

interested in knowing me when we first met, but I didn't listen. I should have respected her opinion and moved on.

I closed my eyes from the bacchanal calling itself a parade marching before my eyes and tried to make sense out of the thoughts rushing through my brain.

It was clear to me now how I had dangerously tied all my success to getting back into my family's life and making my daughter love me. As though that was the only way I would ever find success and redemption.

But it wasn't true. I'd found these things through the help of others and my own willingness to change. So what if I had to continue to admire Ellie's brilliance from afar? Would that be the worst thing in the world? I could keep a scrapbook and gather secondhand news about her from others. And when she was grown and giving speeches at universities or playing concerts in front of thousands of people, who says I couldn't buy myself a ticket and sit in the back and watch like everyone else?

Would that really be so bad?

No one could take away the fact that she was my daughter and always would be a product of me.

And Howie, too, I guess.

I decided then and there that if I had to keep my distance from them to give my little family a happier life, then I would. I'd already led a solitary existence for many years. You could say that I was used to it. And it wasn't like I was really alone. I had Jess and Bill, along with everyone at work. And then there were all The Pet Stop customers, many of whom I had become friendly with and on a first name basis with over the past few weeks.

It started to snow.

Flurries blew down around the lights encircling the crowds of families who cheered and welcomed the white flakes with raised arms.

I decided then that the best thing for me, and everyone, would be for me to go home. I'd slip away and call Flora from the house and make up some excuse for leaving. Then I'd call the following morning and make the same excuse or tell her I wasn't feeling well, and that I wouldn't be able to make Christmas Day.

I admit it was quite a reversal in direction, but I knew in my heart that it was the right thing to do and the best thing for everyone involved, because I felt so calm and at peace with it. And, to be perfectly honest, as much as I loved my daughter, she really did scare me. Maybe in time, as Flora had suggested, Ellie might learn to accept me, and by then I might even be ready to be around her without being terrified of every word that came out of her mouth.

NINETEEN

I slipped away through the crowd without Flora noticing.

I started walking up 2nd Street behind the row of shops. I could still hear the people cheering one street over. I thought about going to The Drowning Pig to see Jess, but then thought better of it. She'd ask why I wasn't with Flora.

As I continued up the street, a strange feeling came over me. I felt suddenly very grown up, like I had finally become a man. I could see that this wasn't the end of the world. I was starting a new life.

The truth is, I couldn't help but think that I had just avoided some great disaster. For once, I'd taken the right path, the smart path, and I was grateful.

It was a beautiful night. The slowly falling snow glistened in the light from the old streetlamps as it gracefully fell onto the peaceful earth. As I continued to walk, I heard the crowd's roars coming from Main Street getting louder. I presumed the parade must have progressed to the part where Santa had arrived on the firetruck, and everyone was losing it for the guy. But it seemed too early for that, I thought, knowing that the parade was supposed to go on for at least another half an hour.

It wasn't until I'd made it to the end of the block and looked up the road towards Main Street that I realized something else completely was going on. For one thing, the cheering wasn't so much cheering, but more like screaming, and I could now see the crowds looking like they were running for their lives.

I bolted up the street to see what was causing the mania.

That's when I saw her, jogging up the middle of Main Street. Her head was covered in Christmas lights and decorations she'd obviously run through on her journey from the garage into town.

Yes, it was Poppy. And she appeared to be in a very bad mood.

How she'd gotten out I had no idea. Having little time to contemplate the subject, I ran in her direction.

As I headed towards her, moving in the opposite way from everyone else who was fleeing her presence, I hadn't a clue what I was doing or how I was going to stop her. It's not like a runaway horse in the movies where you just hold up your hands and say, *Whoa girl, slow down there!* Or jump on her back and pull up on the reins. She had no reins. And she was a hippo. I'd never seen anyone ever ride a hippo except for in cartoons. I'm pretty sure those hippos could talk.

As I got closer to Poppy, I stopped to assess the situation. I watched as she changed direction and headed for the VIP stands. Luckily, all the VIPs had already run off, because with only a simple swipe of her butt, Poppy caused the entire structure to collapse in on itself.

I racked my brain trying to figure out what I could do to calm her down, but nothing came to me. I watched as she headed across the street towards a display of themed desserts, laid out on a line of tables on the sidewalk. This was the baked goods contest held every year. Poppy's large frame didn't miss a single display, trashing every one. Colorful Christmas-themed cakes and pies, along with their blue ribbons, splattered on the sidewalk and got trampled under her feet. She sniffed the remnants and, appearing displeased, moved on towards the snowman-building area.

Once she got to the snowmen and leveled everything in sight, she paused to look around.

Suddenly, I was being pushed aside by several of the news crews who had shown up. Frantically, they set up their cameras to get the best shots of the devastation. Field reporters screamed at their cameramen as they patched into already-scheduled holiday programming for live feeds of the tragic Christmas event taking place.

It dawned on me that this was quickly becoming a spectacle.

I took off and ran behind Poppy, helplessly watching the destruction take place in front of me. I could see the terror and confusion on the townspeople's faces as she ran past them and they either froze or ran for cover. The only difference between them and me was that I was slightly less confused as to how such a horrendous disaster had come about.

What devilish work is this? They must have thought. *What kind of demon from hell has been sent to ruin Christmas?!*

I watched as Poppy stopped at an intersection. She paused and looked inside one of the store windows. It was like she was considering what direction to continue her tour of destruction. She then turned and ran up the street.

I resumed following behind her as she headed towards the giant snow angels in the park next to the bank. With the stores being overcrowded, many townsfolk had fled to the park and into the giant nativity scene, where they hid behind the animals and wise men.

I watched as Poppy stopped in front of the nativity.

I could see Flora and Ellie, along with her grandparents and other town members, trapped in the back, staring out at Poppy with terror in their eyes.

At first, I couldn't understand why Poppy had stopped where she had. And then I saw it. Sitting next to the baby Jesus, someone had left a large basket of fresh fruit, a bountiful gift for the holy child.

Assuming Poppy was moments away from rushing the scene and bringing the whole place down, I ran into the display and in front of Poppy. Then, placing my body between her and the baby Jesus and my family, I grabbed a melon out of the basket and held it high for Poppy to see.

"Look here, girl," I said, careful not to use her real name so as not to give myself away.

She looked right at me, and our eyes met. I was taking a chance that she might recognize her fellow roomie from the night before and that the moments we'd shared back in my garage had touched her and were still fresh in her mind.

Her eyes then left mine and went to the melon.

I slowly walked out of the nativity scene, careful not to knock the baby Jesus out of his little bed.

Poppy's head followed me and the melon all the way. I seemed to now have her full, undivided attention.

Standing on the sidewalk, I rolled the melon into the street, away from the nativity scene and my trapped family. Poppy wasted no time in taking the bait and jumped towards the melon. She quickly scooped it up into her mouth off the sidewalk, her powerful jaws and teeth pulverizing it to bits in seconds.

Flora realized what I was doing and made her way to the basket where she grabbed two melons. She held them up.

"Here, Eddie, catch!" she shouted as she tossed me the fruit over Poppy's head.

I caught them both and held them up in front of Poppy's face. Her eyes clocked the melons immediately and she made a snorting sound.

I started to walk backward, hoping she would follow me. She didn't move.

I set a melon down in the middle of the street and moved away. Poppy then rushed forward and gobbled it up. Flora then tossed me another melon, and I caught it.

"That's the last one!" she shouted.

"It's okay," I called back. "I have a plan."

Khan's grocery store was located less than a hundred feet away from where I stood, two doors down from The Pet Stop. Like most of the shops on the street, Khan's stayed open on Christmas Eve. Khan also, usually, kept his fruit display out in front of the store until the parade was over. I just had to entice Poppy over there and get her occupied by the fruit until the authorities showed up.

I continued to wave the melons in the air so Poppy could see them. She picked up the scent, snorted one more time, then started to move slowly towards me. She paused a few times to look around at the crowd, who were watching from inside the shops, or at least a safe distance up the street.

She then moved forward once again in my direction.

The plan was working. I was getting her closer to the target. I set the last two melons down, equal distance between her and Khan's fruit stand, and stepped away just as she lunged forward and gobbled them up.

I then watched as she raised her snout in the air and picked up the scent of Khan's fruit.

And that was all it took.

Within seconds, and in a rather un-lady-like manner, she made a dash up to the fruit stand, and everyone in town watched as that giant mouth of hers started pulverizing everything in sight.

As I stood there between my hippo and the crowd, the camera crews cautiously moved in around me.

It's all a bit hazy, but I remember microphones being shoved in my face, and several very excitable reporters asking me lots of questions that were making me out to be some kind of local hero.

But all I could think about was how I had caused all this chaos, and nobody knew it.

Suddenly, I recognized Deputy Dan standing next to me, along with two people wearing Animal Services uniforms.

Dan patted me on the back and said, "Good work, Eddie. We got it from here."

It was surreal to watch them move in towards Poppy with their tranquilizer guns. I had a flashback to Howie being arrested for stealing the toaster and had an urge to stop them.

But I didn't.

They shot Poppy in the butt. I watched as the drug took effect immediately, and she started to get drowsy. She snorted and made a loud moan, then laid down. Her heavy head then dropped into the fruit stand, crushing it to the ground. She gave another loud half-sigh, half-moan, then closed her eyes. It was a little sad to watch, even though I knew she really wasn't hurt. The truth was she was safe now and in the hands of professionals who would care for her far better than I could.

I heard Dan say something about zoo officials being on their way, and then I saw Tommy standing behind him. He had just walked up. It was strange seeing the two of them next to each other, knowing that Tommy was the man Dan had been looking for all these years. I watched as Tommy, acting quite nervous, winked at me, as though he were trying to give me a message. He then turned around and disappeared into the crowd as they began to emerge from their hiding places to see the now subdued behemoth that had laid waste to their shiny, glittery world.

I turned to my right and saw Flora standing ten feet away from me. She was also staring at Poppy with a look of absolute confusion and wonder like everyone else.

It was then that I glanced down and saw Ellie standing there at Flora's side. But she wasn't looking at Poppy or at the chaos and destruction all around. She was staring at me. Our eyes met, and I could see immediately she knew what I had done.

Some people might think that, in that moment, I may have felt some validation, knowing that my daughter now knew I had performed a miracle and kept up my end of our deal. But, standing there, in the midst of all that destruction I had caused, that's not how I felt at all. As I stared back at Ellie, all I felt was more embarrassment and shame.

I didn't know what to say to her. So, I just shrugged and smiled pathetically.

I then turned and headed home.

TWENTY

When I got back to the house, I could tell someone had been there. Later, I would learn that Tommy's wink in town was his way of trying to tell me that they had already been to my place and scrubbed it of all evidence. It turns out the moment he and Gretchen saw Poppy from the VIP stands at the parade, they made a beeline to their SUV and drove straight up to the house. They then removed all evidence of the hippo, including lowering the garage door back into place, which Poppy had pushed open, easily breaking the lock, when she ran out of fruit.

Fresh flurries of snow that night took care of Poppy's tracks from the garage all the way to Main Street. Any other time of year, at least a hundred people would have seen Poppy walking from my house into town, but everyone was at the parade that night and not a single witness ever came forward.

Later that evening, when Flora called to ask me where I'd gone, I braced myself for the possibility that Ellie might have told her what I'd done. But from her pleasant tone, it was clear she hadn't. At least not yet. We talked about how crazy the night had been and even laughed about it. She told me how proud she was of me for stopping the hippo's rampage. She said that the entire town was now calling me a hero, and that the whole thing was on the news and that I should turn it on and see it myself.

She then asked if I was coming for Christmas the next day. I told her that I wasn't feeling well and didn't know if I'd make it. She seemed sad but said she'd understand if I didn't.

That night when I went to bed on the couch, I was surprised at how calm I was. I really had no idea how the future was going to unfold. I was at Ellie's mercy more than ever now, but it didn't seem to bother me. I'd made peace with myself. I would move on with my life as planned, not forcing anything, just being grateful for what I had already been given.

What others did was up to them.

I fell asleep immediately and slept through the night.

***

Within a few days, it looked like we were all in the clear regarding the theft of Poppy. As I had expected, there was little investigation into her removal from the zoo other than a few local fraternities being questioned by the authorities.

I must admit, at first, I was a little surprised that Ellie never turned me in to the sheriff. This had been the perfect opportunity for her to finally rid herself of me for good. And I wouldn't have blamed her for it if she had. But she was a clever girl and knew she held in her hands a literal *Go directly to jail card* and wisely kept it close to her.

Granted, her silence might have had something to do with Poppy's ultimate outcome. The video of Poppy's rampant parade destruction had gone viral and had been picked up by news outlets all around the world. In just a few hours, Poppy had become an international phenomenon. Suddenly, everyone on the planet was in love with this one little hippo that, only the night before, had been unknown and unwanted—*hippona non grata*, as Greg liked to call her.

The famous San Diego Wild Animal Park even became aware of the situation and, recognizing an amazing opportunity for publicity when they saw one, offered to take Poppy, and put her in their fancy fifty-acre enclosure. There, she could run wild and play with the other hippos.

Within twenty-four hours of the parade, Poppy was on a specialized train, in her own heated car, filled with all the melons she could eat and on her way to sunny, Southern California.

It was projected that Poppy's addition to the park would triple attendance within six months.

So, I really did save Poppy after all.

And as for the relationship between me, Flora, and Ellie, well, it turns out Ellie never told her mother about my role in Poppy's theft.

The change between all of us happened gradually. Not overnight or even over several months, but over a series of years.

You can't earn someone's trust in an evening; it takes time. Sometimes, a lifetime.

Ellie is now in her late twenties. She's married

and is a successful lawyer working as an advocate for children's rights in Washington. She finally did learn to see me as a father, and we did spend time together, going to movies and museums and such.

Flora and I continued to see each other after that Christmas but kept it casual for a while as I needed to grow and learn to stand on my own.

At one point, after a few years went by, I moved in with her and sold the old house, but by that time, Ellie had already gone off to college at the young age of sixteen.

Eventually, Greg and Anton moved away, too, leaving town for greener, as well as more interesting, pastures. After Wayne retired, he sold me the store, but by that time, he had turned part of it into a year-round Christmas shop. Since the famous parade fiasco with Poppy had become internationally known, half a million people a year now came to visit our little town to see the place where Poppy the hippo destroyed Main Street. Christmas items, especially hippo related, flew off the shelves.

It didn't hurt sales that the man who everyone thought had saved the town from total disaster was working behind the register.

Secretly, also, the man who caused it.

Flora continued to work at the bank, climbing up to bank manager just under Gretchen, who had become bank president when her father retired.

Gretchen and I rarely spoke, although every year I'd send her and Tommy a Christmas card with a hippo on it. I only did it because I got a kick out of imagining her quickly ripping it up and throwing it into the fire to hide the evidence. (Good luck burning all these books!)

I have continued Wayne's tradition of hiring young people who are trying to get on the straight and narrow. But now we close for the whole week before Christmas, and Flora, Ellie, her husband, and I fly as a family to San Diego to visit our hippo at the zoo. Ellie and I grab a box of Cracker Jacks and watch Poppy play in the warm California sun. We've never once spoken about the incident. But I like to think that she must have been impressed that I got her the gift she'd asked for, even if she was just trying to get rid of me at the time.

As for Dan, he retired early due to the stress of the job, and we eventually became good friends. Now he and I play checkers every weekend over a barrel in front of the store.

We don't really say much but I keep him on his toes by letting him think that I cheat, challenging him to catch me.

Sometimes Tommy joins us.

Regarding my views on Christmas, I guess you could say they have changed over the years. I do believe that the epiphany I had that fateful night, before Poppy rampaged the town, captured somewhat the spirit behind the holiday, that life just feels and works better when we check our personal agenda at the door and become more focused on giving than receiving.

I think that's what Christmas was originally supposed to be about.

Or at least should be.

But I can still do without the music.

The End

NOVEL
COMICS

9 798989 409204